Rising Out Of The Pit

Lessons From The Life Of Joseph

By
Bob Yandian

Harrison House
Tulsa, OK

19 18 17 16   10 9 8 7 6 5 4 3 2 1

Rising Out of the Pit
978-168031-031-3
Copyright © 2016 by Bob Yandian

Published by Harrison House Publishers
Tulsa, Oklahoma 74145
www.harrisonhouse.com

Contents

Introduction

Chapter 1   All Things Work Together 1

Chapter 2   When The Bottom Falls Out.............................23

Chapter 3   From The Frying Pan To The Fire.....................37

Chapter 4   From The Pit To The Throne 51

Chapter 5   Reaping What You Sow 67

Chapter 6   The Return To Egypt...81

Chapter 7   The Blessing Overflowing..................................97

Chapter 8   The Elder Shall Serve The Younger...................115

Chapter 9   Jacob's Final Words To His 12 Sons 133

Chapter 10   The Bones Of Joseph...165

About The Author 181

Introduction

The Bible is filled with stories that seem to be "over the top." Although they are true, they are far beyond anything you could imagine. Have you been swallowed by a whale? Jonah was. Have you had marriage problems like David and Bathsheba did? Are you facing a problem as big as the Red Sea and being chased by an army from Egypt? The reason the Bible has stories of this magnitude is to let you know your problem isn't so big. And if God could deliver Moses, David, and Jonah, He can deliver you.

So it is with the story of Joseph. Betrayed by his brothers over two dreams, sold into slavery to get rid of him, entering Egypt as a slave, being wrongly thrown into prison, and finally ending up in a dungeon, Joseph gives us a story far beyond what the average Christian will ever go through. Yet, if God could deliver Joseph and turn his cursing into blessing, He can deliver you. Your financial failures, marriage problems, terminal sickness, or pending lawsuit can be turned around by the God of Joseph.

Are you ready for your cursing to be turned into blessing? Then join me in studying the life of one of the biggest heroes in the Bible. Your faith and courage will be strengthened as you find hope in the reactions of Joseph to the assaults of Satan and people. Your God is bigger than them both.

Chapter 1

All Things Work Together

J oseph is one of the most beloved characters in the Bible. A
young man filled with dreams from God, favored by his father,
betrayed by his brothers, and sold into slavery, he never took his
eyes off God or His promise. He did not allow his heart to become
bitter against his brothers or his circumstances. Joseph would not
be distracted from the vision God had planted in his heart. The
message of Joseph is such a simple message. In this world, difficult
situations confront us all. Whether our problems are seemingly
insignificant or overwhelmingly daunting, God cares and is *the
way* to overcome.

Romans 8:28 is frequently used completely out of context.
Maybe a tornado destroys someone's home and well-intending
people say, "Well, 'all things work together for good'!" implying
God sent the tornado that just demolished their home or maybe
someone becomes sick, and in an attempt to lend comfort someone
says, "Well, 'all things work together for good'! God has some
divine purpose in what He's doing." Unfortunately, many people
in ministry and religious and denominational circles forget about
the influence of Satan and his demons.

The Word of God teaches us that God does *not* send sickness, disease, poverty, or troubles and trials. His desire is for us to be delivered from these things! However, while we're in this world, Jesus said we would have tribulation (John 16:33).

When we are confronted with difficulties in life, all of us are tempted to question God. We have trouble on the job and think, "I prayed and know God gave me this job, so why am I having problems at work?" Satan does not want us to be in the will of God; he will oppose us to get us out of the will of God through discouragement, bitterness, or envy. The devil will do all we allow him to do to keep us from fulfilling the will of God.

The Old Testament is filled with story after story of people who experienced intense opposition, far more challenging than most of us will ever experience, but each story reveals God's faithfulness to deliver those who trust in Him.

David's example is one of my favorites to look to for encouragement. In whatever area of life we may be facing problems, it is almost certain that what David faced was greater. You may think your marital problems are impossible. David impregnated another man's wife, had her husband killed, and the son born to her died. Is someone angry with you? David was walking in God's will, yet the entire nation rose up against him. You say, "I've had trouble with the authorities." Saul's entire military force chased David through the desert, yet David wrote in the Psalms, ". . . though a host encamp against me, I will not fear."

When We Know And When
We Do Not Know How To Pray

Roman 8:28 says, "And we know that all things work together for good to those who love God, to those who are the called according to His purpose."

Notice the first three words, "And we know . . ." The Bible promises all things *can* work together for our good, but it is dependent upon what we know. We cannot interpret verse 28 out of context; it must be read in the context of the rest of the chapter.

There are two types of prayers available to us when we face tribulation: prayer for attacks in areas for which we *do know* how to pray and prayer for attacks in areas for which we *do not know* how to pray. There are times we are caught off guard by the attacks of the enemy and blindsided by Satan. When we do not know how to pray, the Holy Spirit makes intercession for us!

> *Likewise the Spirit also helps in our weaknesses. For we do not know what we should pray for as we ought, but the Spirit Himself makes intercession for us with groanings which cannot be uttered. Now He who searches the hearts knows what the mind of the Spirit is, because He makes intercession for the saints according to the will of God.*
> *Romans 8:26-27*

We can pray with the Spirit, or we can pray with the understanding. In both cases, we're covered! Either way, God will deliver us!

The Hinge: And We Know

The hinge of the entire chapter of Romans 8 is verse 28, "And we know. . . ." Knowledge is extremely important. All things do not work together for good for every Christian, only for those who know something. Verse 28 is simply saying, when we know the plan of God, when we know we love the Lord, when are following as closely to Him as humanly possible, then all things will work together for our good. What this verse does not say is all things in life are good; some things are not good, but God has the ability to blend the good and bad things of life and cause them to advance us.

When struggling with opposition in life, people in the world, and even many Christians, have said, "I've had a setback." However, setbacks do not exist when we are walking in the will of God; tribulations can propel us forward.

Joseph's life demonstrates this truth. Everything that appeared as a setback in his life, God turned around to result in his advancement. When we are in the will of God, we cannot regress. It doesn't matter what the circumstances look like, we can only advance! God has the unique ability to take both the good and bad things and cause us to move forward!

Conditional And Unconditional Promises Of God

Conditional Promises

Aside from the amount of time dedicated in the Bible to

describing the life of Abraham, the longest story in the book of Genesis is about the life of Joseph. Joseph's life story demonstrates both the conditional and the unconditional promises of God. Romans 8:28 is an example of a conditional promise; there are some conditions required before it comes to pass. All things do not work together for the good of every Christian, only those who have knowledge and act upon it. Psalm 1:1 says, "*Blessed is the man . . . ,*" but not every man is blessed. Prerequisites to that promise follow: "...who walks not in the counsel of the ungodly nor stands in the path of sinners nor sits in the seat of the scornful; but his delight is in the law of the LORD, and is His law he meditates day and night" (vv. 1-2). This is the man who is "blessed." Luke 6:38 says, "Give, and it will be given to you." This is also a conditional promise. The preceding verse presents the conditions for the fulfillment of the promise: "Judge not," "condemn not," and "forgive."

Unconditional Promises

Unconditional promises from God cannot be altered. These promises will come to pass regardless of our actions or decisions. One unconditional promise is the second coming of Jesus. Regardless of what man, Satan or his demons try to do to stop it, Jesus is coming back "in a moment, in the twinkling of an eye, at the last trumpet" (1 Corinthians 15:52).

Joseph learned the difference between the conditional and unconditional promises of God. He not only learned to walk with God, he learned obedience before God.

Four Principles Found In The Life Of Jospeh

The first principle we learn from the life of Joseph is that God is *always* faithful, even when we are not. God's faithfulness is not based on our faithfulness to Him. God is faithful when we are well and when we are attacked by sickness or disease. God is faithful whether we are prosperous or in lack. God's faithfulness is not based on us! God is faithful to His own Word and character.

The second principle is God can turn every cursing into blessing for the believer who understands and knows how to apply the Word of God. Satan sends curses, but God can turn them into blessings. This is the whole essence of Romans 8:28, which will be dramatically demonstrated in the life of Joseph.

The third principle, patience, is the ingredient that causes the promises of God to produce in our lives. Hebrews 6:12 tells us to, "imitate those who through faith and patience inherit the promises."

Finally, a faithful believer can cause blessings to come upon both the carnal believers and unbelievers around him. When you are faithful to God, not only are you blessed but those blessings extend to those around you. In 1 Corinthians 7:14 we are told that a believing mate can sanctify an unbelieving mate, and this verse also says their children are holy because of the believing parent. This principle is true throughout the Word of God. Businesses belonging to unbelievers can be blessed in the natural simply because of the presence of a believer. We will see this principle demonstrated in the life of Joseph. Even though his brothers were carnal believers who sold him into slavery and into the house of an unbeliever, all were blessed because of Joseph's faithfulness. In fact, an entire nation benefitted from Joseph's presence.

One Who Crossed The River

From Adam until the time of Abraham, the Gentiles were the only race on earth. Because there was only one race, there was only one language. When Abraham became a believer, he was changed from a Gentile into a Jew or Hebrew. The word *Hebrew* means "one who crossed the river," and that is what Abraham did. Through Abraham, the Jewish race was born, the only race that is both natural and spiritual. Abraham became God's first missionary. He was sent out by God from his home country to a place he did not know. Hebrews 11:8 says, "By faith Abraham obeyed when he was called to go out to the place which he would receive as an inheritance. And he went out, not knowing where he was going."

The time period of Israel extends from Genesis chapter 12 through the Gospels. From Abraham to Moses is the period of the Patriarchs. From Moses to the Lord Jesus Christ is the period of the Law. Joseph is the last of the Patriarchs. Before Joseph was sold as a slave, the children of Israel lived in Canaan. During a famine, Jacob and his sons moved to Egypt. Following Joseph's death, the children of Israel entered a 400-year period during which they became slaves in Egypt before Moses was raised up as their deliverer. The book of Exodus describes the story of Joshua leading the children of Israel back to Canaan, the "Promised Land."

Overview Of The Life Of Joseph

The story of Joseph begins in Genesis chapter 37 with his father Jacob.

Now Jacob dwelt in the land when his father was a stranger, in the land of Canaan.

Genesis 37:1

Now Jacob dwelt in the land when his father was a stranger, in the land of Canaan.

Blessing Of The Firstborn Stolen

The first principle we will discuss is that all things can work together for good.

Jacob's father was Isaac. Jacob had a twin brother named Esau. Most of us would have preferred Esau over Jacob if we had met them because Jacob was a swindler. The reason Jacob was blessed and Esau was not had nothing to do with the difference in their personalities or character. Jacob's name meant "chiseler," and he was always searching for ways to cheat others to benefit himself. Man looks at the outward appearance, but God looks at the heart. Even before they were born, God said of Jacob and Esau, "*Jacob have I loved, Esau have I hated.*" Before they were born, God looked on the hearts of Jacob and Esau and saw there would come a time when Esau would reject the lordship of Jesus Christ and Jacob, even though a swindler, when confronted with the gospel, would receive Jesus as his Lord.

Esau sold his birthright to Jacob for a bowl of lentil stew. Genesis 25:34 (ESV) says, "Then Jacob gave Esau bread and lentil stew, and he ate and drank and rose and went his way. Thus Esau despised his birthright."

In Genesis 27, one of the most familiar stories about Jacob is recounted. Jacob's father, Isaac was old and nearly blind. Isaac called Esau and asked him to hunt for wild game and prepare his favorite meal. In verse 4 Isaac told Esau, "prepare for me delicious food, such as I love, and bring it to me so that I may eat, that my soul may bless you before I die" (ESV).

As Isaac was speaking to Esau, Rebekah, Esau's mother, was listening. After Esau left to hunt, Rebekah relayed what she heard to Jacob. They devised a scheme to deceive Isaac and steal the blessing of the firstborn. Rebekah prepared a meal for Jacob. She put the skins of goats on Jacob's hands and neck and sent him to his father with the stew. Because Jacob didn't sound like Esau, Isaac asked him to come near so he could feel his hands. When he felt the goat hair on Jacob's hands and smelled the aroma of outdoors on him, Isaac blessed him with the blessing of the firstborn.

Hatred Grows In The Hearts Of Joseph's Brothers

Now Jacob dwelt in the land where his father was a stranger, in the land of Canaan. This is the history of Jacob. Joseph, being seventeen years old, was feeding the flock with his brothers. And the lad was with the sons of Bilhah and the sons of Zilpah, his father's wives; and Joseph brought a bad report of them to his father. Now Israel (Jacob) loved Joseph more than all his children, because he was the son of his old age. Also he made him a tunic of many colors. (explanation mine)

Genesis 37:1-3

Joseph was the youngest of his brothers, yet his father gave him authority over his older brothers and he brought a bad report about them to his father. Verse 2 says, "And the lad was with the sons of Bilhah and the sons of Zilpah." The sons of Bilhah were Dan and Naphtali. The sons of Zilpah were Gad and Asher.

Verse 3 states very clearly that Jacob loved Joseph more than any of his other sons. This fact combined with Joseph bringing to his father a report about his brothers every day, even though the reports were true, was the recipe for envy, anger, and resentment.

Jacob made a mistake in showing partiality toward Joseph over his other sons. His partiality bred bitterness in Joseph's brothers. They grew to hate Joseph. One way Jacob demonstrated his partiality was by making Joseph a special coat of many colors. Most of us have seen images of what others imagine Joseph's many colored coat may have looked like with reds and purples and other vibrant colors. However, the Hebrew says the coat had long sleeves and it was a symbol of authority representing Joseph's authority over his brothers. Every time his brothers saw him coming toward them wearing his coat, it was a reminder of his authority over them.

But when his brothers saw that their father loved him more than all his brothers, they hated him and could not speak peaceably to him.

Genesis 37:4

The hatred of Joseph's brothers toward him began here. First John 3:15 says, "Whoever hates his brother is a murderer." Because Joseph's brothers hated him, they were guilty of mental murder, which manifests later in the story.

How did hatred build in the hearts of Joseph's brothers?

And his brothers said to him, "Shall you indeed reign over us? Or shall you indeed have dominion over us?" So they hated him even more for his dreams and for his words.

Genesis 37:8

Notice what happened in the middle of verse 8: "they hated him even more." Sometimes an individual may feel justified in hating, but hatred is opposite of the love of God. If we allow bitterness to fester in us for what seems unfair, God will hold us accountable. But if we determine to walk in love, even if something is unjust, God will turn it around for our good.

If we allow hatred and mental sins in our lives, God will not work all things together for our good. Regardless of attacks from the world or Satan or the circumstances confronting us, when we walk in love toward those around us, there is no such thing as a setback.

Verse 11 says, "And his brothers envied him." The resentment of Joseph's brothers toward him grew worse.

Thought Sins To Action Sins

Verse 18 says, "Now when they saw him afar off, even before

11

he came near to them, they conspired against him to kill him."

Verses 19 and 20 say, "Then they said to one another, 'Look this dreamer is coming! Come therefore, let us now kill him and cast him into some pit; and we shall say, "Some wild beast has devoured him." We shall see what will become of his dreams!'"

Joseph's brothers' sin had grown from thoughts of hatred toward him to actually planning to murder him and how they would cover up his death. The sin had gone from thoughts to words being spoken out of their mouths.

Proverbs 23:7 says, "For as he thinks in his heart, so *is* he."

Matthew 12:34 says, "For out of the abundance of the heart the mouth speaks."

Notice again what the brothers said in verse 19, "Look, this dreamer is coming!" What was in their hearts had now been given voice; they were beginning to mock Joseph. In verse 20, they verbalized what they planned in their hearts to put into action: "We will kill him and then we will see what becomes of his dreams!"

Back in verse 4, it said, "But when his brothers saw that their father loved him more than all his brothers, they hated him and could not speak peaceably to him." From verse 4 on, Joseph's brothers did not address him cordially; there was no peaceable conversation between them. It is likely some of us have been in a similar situation where there was an invisible wall hindering communication between another person and us, and regardless of what we said to assuage the block in communication, the problem was not solved.

Joseph's Dreams

Verses 5-10 of Genesis 37 describe the two dreams Joseph had. In these dreams, God would confirm to Joseph ahead of time what he would be facing; in essence, these dreams were God's Word to Joseph because there was no Bible available to him. God's Word to Joseph came through his dreams.

Now Joseph had a dream, and he told it to his brothers; and they hated him even more. So he said to them, "Please hear this dream which I have dreamed: There we were, binding sheaves in the field. Then behold, my sheaf arose and also stood upright; and indeed your sheaves stood all around and bowed down to my sheaf." And his brothers said to him, "Shall you indeed reign over us? Or shall you indeed have dominion over us?" So they hated him even more for his dreams and for his words. Then he dreamed still another dream and told it to his brothers, and said, "Look, I have dreamed another dream. And this time, the sun, the moon, and the eleven stars bowed down to me." So he told it to his father and his brothers; and his father rebuked him and said to him, "What is this dream that you have dreamed? Shall your mother and I and your brothers indeed come to bow down to the earth before you?" And his brothers envied him, but his father kept the matter in mind.

Genesis 37:5–11

The dreams God gave to Joseph only fueled the negative feelings his brothers already had toward him. The first dream indicated Joseph's brothers would bow down to him. The next dream indicated his entire family and the whole nation of Israel would bow down to him.

In describing the second dream, Joseph said in verse 9, "The sun, the moon, and the eleven stars bowed down to me." The sun represented Joseph's father, Jacob. The moon represented Joseph's mother, Rachel. Notice, there were eleven stars, which represented Joseph's brothers, but at this point in the recounting of Joseph's life, there were only ten brothers: Rueben, Simeon, Levi, Judah, Issachar, and Zebulun, who were the sons of Leah; Dan and Naphtali, who were the sons of Bilhah; and Gad and Asher, who were the sons of Zilpah. So why were there eleven stars bowing down to Joseph in his dream? When the fulfillment of the second dream finally came to pass, there was one more son who had been born to Jacob, Benjamin.

As Joseph recounted the second dream, it made his brothers angry and upset his father. Jacob rebuked Joseph but did not dismiss the dream and purposed to remember it. Verse 11 says, "And his brothers envied him, but his father kept the matter *in mind.*" Jacob did not understand Joseph's dream but did not dismiss it. One of the best things we can do when we don't understand something is put it on the shelf; that is exactly what Jacob did.

This dream will become very important. Because it was recounted to Joseph's brothers before they betrayed him, the will of God was revealed to them concerning Joseph. Before Jacob mourned what he believed to be Joseph's death, he had heard the will of God as Joseph shared his dreams with him. How was it possible for Joseph to be dead, as Jacob believed at one point in this story, if Jacob, his wife, and his eleven sons were to bow down to Joseph? How could this promise from God come to pass if Joseph was actually dead? When Joseph's brothers told their father Joseph was dead, he believed their story over what God had promised through Joseph's dreams.

In fact, Jacob would carry this grief in his heart until he was finally reunited with Joseph many years later, because he believed the report of his sons rather than the promise of God. How often do we do the same as Jacob? We look at the circumstances rather than keeping our eyes fixed on the promises of God.

Joseph Searches For His Brothers

Then his brothers went to feed their father's flock in Shechem. And Israel said to Joseph, "Are not your brothers feeding the flock in Shechem? Come, I will send you to them." So he said to him, "Here I am." Then he said to him, "Please go and see if it is well with your brothers and well with the flocks, and bring back word to me." So he sent him out of the Valley of Hebron, and he went to Shechem.

Genesis 37:12-14

Verse 12 says Joseph's brothers were in Shechem feeding their father's flock and his father sent him to check on them. The name

Shechem means "shoulder" or "strength". The reason Joseph's father sent him was because he didn't trust that his other sons were caring for his sheep properly.

> *Now a certain man found him, and there he was, wandering in the field. And the man asked him, saying, "What are you seeking?" So he said, "I am seeking my brothers. Please tell me where they are feeding their flocks." And the man said, "They have departed from here, for I heard them say, 'Let us go to Dothan.'" So Joseph went after his brothers and found them in Dothan.*
>
> *Genesis 37:15-17*

Dothan was a desert area. Why would the brothers have their father's sheep in the desert? They were not thinking about the sheep. They were thinking about themselves.

Joseph Finds His Brothers In Dothan

> *Now when they saw him afar off, even before he came near them, they conspired against him to kill him.*
>
> *Genesis 37:18*

Joseph's brothers hated him so intensely, they devised a plan to kill him as he approached them. God's will had already been revealed to them. First, the brothers would bow down to Joseph. Next, the entire family would bow down to him. Joseph's brothers were trying to change the will of God but even though they were unfaithful, God is faithful and His plan *will* come to pass! Even ten brothers scheming against one man could not alter the will of God.

Then they said to one another, "Look, this dreamer is coming!"

Genesis 37:19

As they watched Joseph approaching, they spoke of him with ridicule and sarcasm.

The Plot Against Joseph

"Come therefore, let us now kill him and cast him into some pit; and we shall say, 'Some wild beast has devoured him.' We shall see what will become of his dreams!" But Reuben heard it, and he delivered him out of their hands, and said, "Let us not kill him." And Reuben said to them, "Shed no blood, but cast him into this pit which is in the wilderness, and do not lay a hand on him"— that he might deliver him out of their hands, and bring him back to his father.

Genesis 37:20-22

Reuben's Plan

Reuben was noble but unstable. He did not want to upset his brothers, but he also did not want to see Joseph die. Reuben devised a plan which is seen in verses 21 and 22. Reuben's plan was to have Joseph put in a pit. The brothers agreed to his plan. The part of the plan he did not share with his brothers was that once his brothers left the area, he would return and rescue Joseph from the pit and deliver him to their father.

So it came to pass, when Joseph had come to his brothers, that they stripped Joseph of his tunic, the tunic of many colors that was on him. Then they took him and cast him into a pit. And the pit was empty; there was no water in it.

And they sat down to eat a meal. Then they lifted their eyes and looked, and there was a company of Ishmaelites, coming from Gilead with their camels, bearing spices, balm, and myrrh, on their way to carry them down to Egypt.

Genesis 37:23-25

Reuben left his brothers for a time, perhaps to check on the sheep. While Reuben was gone, they stripped Joseph of his coat and threw him into the pit, which had no water.

Judah's Plan

Notice how calloused Joseph's brothers had become toward him. Verse 25 says, "And they sat down to eat a meal." While Joseph was in a pit with no water, his brothers sat down outside the pit and began eating a meal!

Genesis 42:21, which is an account years after Joseph was sold into slavery, reveals more about how Joseph felt while he was in the pit. Joseph's brothers traveled to Egypt to buy grain during a famine but had been asked to bring their youngest brother, Benjamin, before they would receive grain. Verse 21 says, "Then they said to one another, 'We *are* truly guilty concerning our brother, for we saw the anguish of his soul when he pleaded with us, and we would not hear; therefore this distress has come upon us.'"

Joseph was down in the pit crying out, pleading with his brothers, but they ignored him and continued eating.

So Judah said to his brothers, "What profit is there if we kill
our brother and conceal his blood? Come and let us sell him
to the Ishmaelites, and let not our hand be upon him, for he
is our brother and our flesh." And his brothers listened. Then
Midianite traders passed by; so the brothers pulled Joseph up
and lifted him out of the pit, and sold him to the Ishmaelites
for twenty shekels of silver. And they took Joseph to Egypt.
Genesis 37:26-28

While they were eating, the brothers looked up and saw Ishmaelite traders headed their direction. Judah convinced his brothers to sell Joseph to the Ishmaelites who were traveling to Egypt to sell spices, medicine, and perfume. They agreed and sold Joseph for twenty pieces of silver. Later, the Ishamelites sold Joseph for thirty pieces of silver to the Egyptians.

Then Reuben returned to the pit, and indeed Joseph was not in
the pit; and he tore his clothes. And he returned to his brothers
and said, "The lad is no more; and I, where shall I go?"
Genesis 37:29-30

When Reuben returned to his brothers, he tore his clothes because Joseph was no longer in the pit. He was probably in despair at the loss of his brother and also at the thought of explaining the situation to his father.

The Brothers Deceive Jacob

So they took Joseph's tunic, killed a kid of the goats, and dipped the tunic in the blood. Then they sent the tunic of many colors, and they brought it to their father and said, "We have found this. Do you know whether it is your son's tunic or not?"

Genesis 37:31-32

The brothers dipped Joseph's coat in the blood of a baby goat they had killed. When they returned home, they showed the coat to their father and asked him to identify it.

And he recognized it and said, "It is my son's tunic. A wild beast has devoured him. Without doubt Joseph is torn to pieces." Then Jacob tore his clothes, put sackcloth on his waist, and mourned for his son many days.

Genesis 37:33-34

Instead of believing God's word about Joseph through the dreams Joseph was given, Jacob immediately believed his sons' lies and believed a wild beast had torn him apart. Just as Jacob had deceived his own father to receive the blessing, his sons now deceived him. Jacob was reaping what he had sown many years before.

The Hypocrisy Of Jacob's Sons

And all his sons and all his daughters arose to comfort him; but he refused to be comforted, and he said, "For I shall go down

into the grave to my son in mourning." Thus his father wept
for him.

Genesis 37:35

Notice the hypocrisy of Jacob's sons. They sold their brother and knew he was not dead, yet they attempted to comfort their father who was in despair because of them. This passage also reveals that Jacob was emotionally unstable and chose to mourn for many years when he could have received comfort.

Now the Midianites had sold him in Egypt to Potiphar, an
officer of Pharaoh and captain of the guard.

Genesis 37:36

No Setbacks In God

Prior to this incident in Joseph's life, he has experienced some good things. His father loved him and made him a special coat because of that love. His father entrusted him to watch over his brothers, and even though his brothers hated him, Reuben had a conscience and tried to rescue him from being killed by his brothers. In one chapter, Joseph's good fortune changed from overseeing his brothers to becoming a slave in Egypt. Things went from good to bad in Joseph's life. Yet even though he became a slave, God chose the best family in the entire nation of Egypt for Joseph to serve. Although it appeared the circumstances in Joseph's life were regressing and the dreams God gave him would not come to pass, all things were working together for his good. Although it looked like Joseph was going the wrong direction, he was actually advancing.

When we are in the will of God, there is no such thing as a setback. Perhaps the situation in which we find ourselves is unjust and undeserved, but when we are serving God, what may seem like a setback God is calling advancement. Although it appeared Joseph's dreams would never come to pass, he would become the prime minister of the entire nation of Egypt. His dreams would come to pass and his brothers would see those dreams manifest. The same God who brought the fulfillment of Joseph's dreams is still working to bring about our dreams today!

Chapter 2

When The Bottom Falls Out

When Joseph's brothers saw Joseph coming toward them in Dothan, they were remembering the dreams God had given him, which is evidenced by their proud statement, "Look, here comes the 'dreamer,'" and the tone of their comments indicated they were thinking, "He thinks we will bow down to him! We'll see what happens to his dreams."

After they put him in a pit with no water, they saw the Ishmaelites coming and decided they would sell him into slavery. I can imagine them thinking to themselves, "We will sell him and at least get some money out of him." Joseph was taken into Egypt, and as far as his brothers were concerned, they would never see him again. In their thinking, Joseph would probably die as a slave.

Through Joseph's two dreams, God was trying to reveal to his brothers the future. When God declares the future, it *will* come to pass. God has a plan for each of our lives. Man cannot destroy God's plan. When we stand on the word God has given us, no matter what man tries to do, that word will come to pass. They tried to do it with Joseph. They tried to do it with the prophets, and they tried to do it with Jesus. But God's Word is true, and it will stand.

Things seemed to be going from bad to worse in Joseph's life, even though he had a word from God. Chapter 39 continues with the story of Joseph.

Potiphar, Captain Of The Guard

Now Joseph had been taken down to Egypt. And Potiphar, an officer of Pharaoh, captain of the guard, an Egyptian, bought him from the Ishmaelites who had taken him down there.

Genesis 39:1

Potiphar's name means "devoted to the sun god." He was a heathen, a sinner. There is no recorded incident or indication that Potiphar accepted the Lord while Joseph served him. Joseph probably witnessed to Potiphar, even by the integrity of his life.

Verse 1 refers to Potiphar as "captain of the guard." Potiphar was a bodyguard to Pharaoh; he was the third or fourth highest ranking man in the entire kingdom. Potiphar's position was high ranking and very important. He was a very wealthy man. It is interesting to note that Joseph wasn't placed as a slave in just an average man's home; he was placed in the home of one of the most influential men in Egypt.

Potiphar saw the nobility of Joseph, and his trust in Joseph grew every day. Eventually, Potiphar entrusted his entire estate to Joseph to run. Even though Joseph was a slave, he had authority over all of the hired servants in Potiphar's house.

The Lord Was With Joseph

The LORD was with Joseph, and he was a successful man; and he was in the house of his master the Egyptian.

And his master saw that the LORD was with him and that the LORD made all he did to prosper in his hand.

Genesis 39:2-3

Potiphar observed two realities in Joseph's life: the Lord was with him and the Lord caused everything Joseph set his hands on to prosper! We don't always need to tell others we are believers. When we walk with God, others should be able to see Him in our lives.

One of the greatest opportunities for testimony a believer can have in his or her life is when asked by a sinner, "What is different about you? I can see a difference in your life compared to others."

The presence of the Lord was with Joseph in a way that Potiphar could literally see there was something different about him. It would have been tempting for Joseph to become bitter after what his brothers had done to him. There were probably slaves working for Potiphar who had become bitter, blaming parents, their upbringing, or anyone or anything else for their current situation. When we face difficult situations in life, it is so easy to place the blame rather than look to the Word of God. Joseph's entire life was devoted to the Lord, and Potiphar could see it in him. The Lord was with Joseph.

Looking further down in this chapter, in verses 21 through 23 it says, "But the LORD was with Joseph and showed him mercy, and He gave him favor in the sight of the keeper in the prison. And the keeper of the prison committed to Joseph's hand all the prisoners who *were* in the prison: whatever they did there, it was his doing. The keeper of the prison did not look into anything *that was* under Joseph's authority, because the LORD was with him; and whatever he did, the LORD made *it* prosper."

When Joseph was sold into slavery by his brothers into a culture totally foreign to his, he probably thought things couldn't get worse. He'd had freedom all of his life, but now he was a slave. But by the end of the chapter, things got worse. He was thrown into prison because of a lie against him. Yet, even while in prison, Joseph rose to the top and became the master over the other prisoners. Joseph was as low as he could possibly be with the exception of death. But even in all of this, the Lord was with Joseph.

Most of us today would probably not have passed the second or third test. Yet, by the time Joseph reached rock bottom, he was still praising the Lord, interpreting dreams, and listening to the voice of the Holy Spirit.

Joseph is a type of Jesus who went to death, hell, and the grave for us; and in a moment of time, God raised Him and made Him to sit at the right hand of the Father. Joseph is also a type of you and me. While we were dead in our trespasses and sins, once we were born again, God raised us up and seated us in heavenly places in Christ Jesus!

> *And his master saw that the LORD was with him and that the LORD made all he did to prosper in his hand.*
>
> *Genesis 39:3*

Deuteronomy 28:8 says, "The Lord will command the blessing on you in your storehouses and in all to which you set your hand, and He will bless you in the land which the Lord your God is giving you."

This promise was exactly what was happening in Joseph's life. Although the natural circumstances looked bad, God was still with Joseph, and anything he did was blessed. Whether it was overseeing the slaves in Potiphar's house or the slaves in prison or being a servant to the other slaves, God was with Joseph.

Our circumstances don't dictate who we are or our relationship with God. We can allow the circumstances of our lives to affect us; or, like Joseph, we can affect our circumstances.

Genesis 39 reveals that Joseph did not allow the circumstances surrounding his life to negatively affect him.

Joseph Learned To Be Content

In Philippians, 4:11 Paul said, "I have learned in whatever state I am, to be content." Contentment is not a feeling. Contentment is learned. Joseph learned to be content regardless of the circumstances confronting him.

No matter what happened to Joseph, he remained the same. If we live according to the circumstances in our lives, we become unstable, ever-changing according to what is happening around us. Joseph was not affected.

So Joseph found favor in his sight, and served him. Then he made him overseer of his house, and all that he had he put under his authority.

Genesis 39:4

Joseph being assigned as overseer meant he was the administrator under Potiphar himself. Although Potiphar's job was training and working with the king's guards, his home was a massive estate. Not only did he have responsibilities in Pharaoh's court, he had responsibilities at home. Potiphar must have observed the gift of administration in Joseph's life.

> *So it was, from the time that he had made him overseer of his house and all that he had, that the LORD blessed the Egyptian's house for Joseph's sake; and the blessing of the LORD was on all that he had in the house and in the field.*
>
> *Genesis 39:5*

Potiphar's Household Blessed Because Of Joseph

Potiphar was a sinner, but he was blessed for Joseph's sake. Because he entrusted his entire household to Joseph, he was blessed. God is able to bless our employers because of our presence, even if we are the only Christian in the entire organization.

> *Thus he left all that he had in Joseph's hand, and he did not know what he had except for the bread which he ate. Now Joseph was handsome in form and appearance.*
>
> *Genesis 39:6*

Potiphar left *all* he had in Joseph's hand! All means all! The only one in a higher position in Potiphar's household was Potiphar himself. The same was true in Jacob's household. The only one higher in position than Joseph was his father, Jacob. It is interesting to note that no matter where Joseph ended up, he became second in command.

Joseph was gifted, but it was because of the Lord's mercy. The gifts Joseph possessed were from the Lord. Potiphar was not worried about anything concerning his home because Joseph handled everything. The more he turned over to Joseph's care, the more blessed he became.

Potiphar's Wife

And it came to pass after these things that his master's wife cast longing eyes on Joseph, and she said, "Lie with me."
Genesis 39:7

Potiphar's wife saw Joseph. He was young, maybe 19 or 20 years old. He was handsome and brilliant. Potiphar was gone during the day with his duties, so she tried to take advantage of the situation by convincing Joseph to go to bed with her.

Joseph's character is revealed in the next passage.

But he refused and said to his master's wife, "Look, my master does not know what is with me in the house, and he has put everything that he has in my charge. There is no one greater in this house than I, nor has he kept back anything from me but you, because you are his wife. How then can I do this great wickedness, and sin against God?"
Genesis 39:8-9

Joseph not only recognized the significance of what Potiphar had entrusted to his care, but he also knew to sin against Potiphar would be sinning against God.

As believers, we need to understand that when people trust us, it is as if God has trusted us. Joseph understood the responsibility of authority. If your boss asks you to do something, and it is not a sin, it is as if the Lord is asking you to do it. In 1 Peter 5:6 we are instructed to, "humble yourselves under the mighty hand of God, that He may exalt you in due time."There are times when our bosses represent the mighty hand of God.

Joseph saw Potiphar's acceptance, trust, and responsibilities assigned to him equal to the Lord's trust in him.

> *So it was, as she spoke to Joseph day by day, that he did not heed her, to lie with her or to be with her.*
> *Genesis 39:10*

Day after day, Potiphar's wife tried to get Joseph to go to bed with her, but every time, Joseph refused.

> *But it happened about this time, when Joseph went into the house to do his work, and none of the men of the house was inside, that she caught him by his garment, saying, "Lie with me." But he left his garment in her hand, and fled and ran outside.*
> *Genesis 39:11-12*

In 1 Corinthians 6:18, we are told, "Flee sexual immorality. Every sin that a man does is outside the body, but he who commits sexual immorality sins against his own body." "Flee" means to run from sexual immorality. This is exactly what Joseph did. When Potiphar's wife grabbed Joseph's garment, he ran out of the house and as he ran, his arms came out of his coat, leaving her with it.

When temptations come, we need to run from them. Thoughts will come, but if they are not in line with God's Word, we need to flee from them. We need to cast down imaginations and every high thing that exalts itself against the knowledge of God!

And so it was, when she saw that he had left his garment in her hand and fled outside, that she called to the men of her house and spoke to them, saying, "See, he has brought in to us a Hebrew to mock us. He came in to me to lie with me, and I cried out with a loud voice. And it happened, when he heard that I lifted my voice and cried out, that he left his garment with me, and fled and went outside."
Genesis 39:13-15

Potiphar's wife called for the men of her house to come so she could accuse Joseph. She began by emphasizing race. "My husband has allowed a Hebrew slave to make a fool of us." By pointing out that Joseph was a Hebrew, she was implying the superiority of the Egyptians. These slaves had worked alongside Joseph and had probably observed his integrity and character. They listened to Potiphar's wife's accusations, but likely knew the type of woman she really was. More than likely Joseph was not the first man in the household she had tried to seduce. She claimed she screamed when Joseph supposedly tried to rape her, but none of the men recalled hearing her scream. As she accused Joseph, I can imagine the men of the household listening but not believing a word she spoke. They kept silent because to side with Joseph would be to lose their jobs and positions as slaves in the household.

So she kept his garment with her until his master came home. Then she spoke to him with words like these, saying, "The Hebrew servant you brought to us came in to me to mock me; so it happened, as I lifted my voice and cried out, that he left his garment with me and fled outside."

Genesis 39:16-18

Potiphar's wife held the garment that supported her lie. She then blamed her husband for bringing a Hebrew into their home. Notice, she accused, *"The Hebrew servant whom **you brought to us**."*

So it was, when his master heard the words which his wife spoke to him, saying, "Your servant did to me after this manner," that his anger was aroused.

Genesis 39:19

Potiphar's Anger Displayed

After hearing his wife's elaborate lie, Potiphar became very angry. He found Joseph and immediately had him thrown into prison. He was so controlled by his anger, Potiphar didn't stop to think that a guilty man would be on the run and Joseph was not. Although Potiphar would have interrogated suspicious people as part of his responsibilities as captain of the guard, in this particular instance, he immediately threw Joseph into prison without any questions, without a trial, without any attempt to find out if Joseph was actually guilty.

After this instance, Potiphar is never mentioned again in the story of Joseph. As long as he blessed Joseph, Potiphar was blessed.

After he unjustly threw Joseph in prison, we don't know what happened to Potiphar. The Bible doesn't say.

God told Abraham in Genesis 12:3, "I will bless those who bless you, and I will curse him who curses you. . . ." This principle still held true in Joseph's time. Potiphar came against one of God's children, and it opened him up to a curse.

> *Then Joseph's master took him and put him into the prison, a place where the king's prisoners were confined. And he was there in the prison.*
> *Genesis 39:20*

This verse does not say Joseph's master chased after him or that they had to send out the military to find him. It just says, "Joseph's master took him and put him into the prison." Joseph was probably working faithfully performing the tasks assigned to him when Potiphar found him.

> *But the LORD was with Joseph and showed him mercy, and He gave him favor in the sight of the keeper of the prison.*
> *Genesis 39:21*

It would have been natural for Joseph to have become upset. There was a calling on his life. He loved the Lord and did not allow the circumstances surrounding his life to cause bitterness in his heart.

Romans 8:28 says, "And we know that all things work together for good to those who love God, to those who are the called according to *His* purpose." God can take even the bad things that happen in our lives and work them out and cause them to be blessings if we'll hearken to the Word of the Lord. If we leave the negative circumstances in God's hands and cast our burden on the Lord, even the bad things in our lives God can turn for our good.

All Things Work Together For Good

And the keeper of the prison committed to Joseph's hand all the prisoners who were in the prison; whatever they did there, it was his doing.
Genesis 39:22

Even in prison, Joseph's integrity could be seen. Regardless of where Joseph was, he rose to the top. Whether in his father's house, a slave in Potiphar's house or a prisoner, Joseph always advanced and became second in command.

The keeper of the prison did not look into anything that was under Joseph's authority, because the LORD was with him; and whatever he did, the LORD made it prosper.
Genesis 39:23

Just as it occurred when Joseph was in Potiphar's house, the keeper of the prison entrusted everything to Joseph's care. Joseph was sold into slavery by his brothers, made a slave in Potiphar's house, entrusted with running Potiphar's entire estate, falsely accused, thrown in prison, and then entrusted by the keeper of the prison with all of those in the prison. Yet in all of this, God was with Joseph. It didn't seem like things could get any worse for Joseph, but they did. The circumstances surrounding Joseph's life continually seemed to deteriorate, yet what remained constant was Joseph's trust in the Lord. Most of us, at this point in the story, would be yelling to whoever would listen, "I've been wronged! I'm innocent!" But Joseph just kept trusting the Lord over and over and over again!

We can either go by our circumstances or go by the Word. If circumstances are screaming, "The Word isn't true," if the demons are shouting in your ear, "The Word isn't true," if Satan himself is sneering, "The Word isn't true," REMEMBER, THE WORD IS TRUE!

"You trusted God and got sold into slavery. You trusted God and got thrown in prison. You thought things couldn't get worse, but they did. There's nowhere to go from here but death. Now what will become of your dreams?" Joseph's mind and imagination probably tried to run wild. The Bible says we are to take every thought into captivity, casting down imaginations and every thought to the obedience of Christ. That is exactly what Joseph did, and as we will see, God blessed him and literally caused those two dreams to come to pass. While Joseph was in that prison, he was probably remembering those two dreams and wondering how God would cause them to come to pass. Yet he continued to trust God.

Has God spoken a word to your heart and yet the circumstances in which you find yourself contradict that word, and it seems you are as far away from its manifestation as you could possibly be? Are you wondering to yourself, "How will God ever cause this to come to pass?" It is not up to you to figure it out; it is up to God to perform it! Your part is to lean on the Lord, trust in His Word, and He will cause it to come to pass!

Chapter 3

From The Frying Pan To The Fire

Suffering is a topic taught in almost every book of the New Testament, especially in 2 Corinthians and Peter's epistles. Suffering in the Christian life is inevitable. However, when we choose to lean on the Lord and trust in Him, we will be delivered from suffering. As certain as the sun rises every morning, as surely as God is alive, we will come out of suffering when we trust in Him.

There is a growing up process in every area of our Christian life, including maturity in suffering. The more we know the promises and power of God, the more we grow in our ability to handle suffering. The essence of the epistles of Peter is how God brings us out of suffering.

Able Ministers

Second Corinthians 3:5-6 (NLT) says, "It is not that we think we are qualified to do anything on our own. Our qualification comes from God. He has enabled us to be ministers of his new covenant. This is a covenant not of written laws, but of the Spirit. The old written covenant ends in death; but under the new covenant, the Spirit gives life."

Not only has God qualified us as ministers but as *able ministers*. Every believer is a fulltime minister of the Gospel. This means whether we are currently in prosperity or not, whether we are currently in health or not, and whether we are currently suffering or not, we are still ministers. Suffering doesn't say, "Time out from ministry. I'll just wait until this suffering passes, and *then* I will go back to ministering." No, we are ministers at all times.

The Source Of All Comfort

In 2 Corinthians 1:3-4 (NLT), it says, "God is our merciful Father and THE SOURCE OF ALL COMFORT. He comforts us in all our troubles so that we can comfort others. When they are troubled, we will be able to give them the same comfort God has given us" (emphasis mine).

This passage says God comforts us in all our troubles. Why does God comfort us? So we will be able to give others the same comfort God has given us. This does not mean we must go through the same trouble another is experiencing to give them the comfort God has given us. Because of God's comfort, we can help anyone going through anything. We must simply reach out.

God never promised He would immediately deliver us from trouble the moment it confronted us. Ephesians 3:10 says, "to the intent that now the manifold wisdom of God might be made known by the church to the principalities and powers in the heavenly *places*." Each time we use the name of Jesus against Satan or endure temptations, tests, and trials, the manifold wisdom of God is revealed through us, the Church. Each time a believer endures problems, God's multi-faceted wisdom is demonstrated to the devil through His Church.

Second Corinthians 1:5-7 (NLT) says, "For the more we

suffer for Christ, the more God will shower us with His comfort through Christ. Even when we are weighed down with troubles, it is for your comfort and salvation! For when we ourselves are comforted, we will certainly comfort you. Then you can patiently endure the same things we suffer. We are confident that as you share in our sufferings, you will also share in the comfort God gives us." When we go through suffering and we are showered with God's comfort, we are able to share God's comfort with others going through troubles.

The ideas, strategies, and craftiness of man cannot stop the plan of God. The plan of God had already been revealed to Joseph's brothers through Joseph's dreams. Instead of accepting God's plan, they made the decision to attempt to control the future; they decided they would discount Joseph's rendition of the plan of God and intervene to ensure it would not ever come to pass.

How often have we thought things are as low as they possibly can go and then the bottom falls out? This is where Genesis 40 begins in the story of the life of Joseph.

The Butler And The Baker

It came to pass after these things that the butler and the baker of the king of Egypt offended their lord, the king of Egypt.
Genesis 40:1

The reason the butler and baker were thrown into prison was because one of them had conspired against the king and tried to poison him. The king did not know which man it was, so he had both of them thrown into prison until he could run an investigation to discover the man who was guilty.

The butler was not a butler in the modern sense of the word. His title was actually chief cupbearer. During Joseph's day, the chief cupbearer was responsible for tasting the wine of the king to be sure it was not poisoned.

The baker was the *chief baker*. Not only did he prepare the food for the king, he oversaw all those who prepared food for the king. Pharaoh didn't have a particular chef; he had many. Similar to the chief cupbearer, as the chief baker, he was responsible to taste the food before the king ate it to be sure it was not poisoned.

In addition to tasting the wine for the king, the cupbearer was responsible for introducing all foreign dignitaries to him. In essence, the chief cupbearer served as the State Department does today. He was required to know the names of those he was introducing to the king; therefore, an excellent memory was required.

> *And Pharaoh was angry with his two officers, the chief butler and the chief baker. So he put them in custody in the house of the captain of the guard, in the prison, the place where Joseph was confined.*
>
> *Genesis 40:2-3*

Even though he isn't mentioned by name, the captain of the guard was Potiphar. Pharaoh put the two men into Potiphar's custody. Potiphar had probably not been to the prison for a long time. But in visiting the prison, he learned it was being run very efficiently. He then discovered Joseph was running the prison.

Joseph Demoted

*And the captain of the guard charged Joseph with them, and
he served them; so they were in custody for a while.*

Genesis 40:4

This verse says, "... *he served them.*"

When Potiphar realized Joseph had oversight of the prison,
he made Joseph a slave to the cupbearer and the baker. It seemed
things couldn't get any worse for Joseph. He had been thrown into
a pit by his brothers, sold into slavery, promoted to manager of
Potiphar's house, then falsely accused of rape by Potiphar's wife,
thrown into prison, made overseer in the prison, and then demoted
to be a slave serving two other prisoners who had just been thrown
into prison by Pharaoh.

It seemed Joseph had reached the lowest of the low. He probably
thought the bottom couldn't drop out again, but it did. At this point,
it had been 11 years since Joseph's brothers threw him in the pit.
Joseph had probably thought back to the dreams in which his
brothers bowed down to him. The fulfillment of those dreams must
have seemed as far away from reality as possible to Joseph. Yet, he
did not let go of what God had promised him. Joseph could have
become bitter toward his brothers or toward God, but he refused
to walk in unforgiveness or to let go of God's promise.

"Why Do You Look So Sad?"

Then the butler and the baker of the king of Egypt, who

were confined in the prison, had a dream, both of them, each man's dream in one night and each man's dream with its own interpretation. And Joseph came in to them in the morning and looked at them, and saw that they were sad. So he asked Pharaoh's officers who were with him in the custody of his lord's house, saying, "Why do you look so sad today?"

Genesis 40:5-7

This passage reveals that the chief cupbearer and the butler were both unhappy, and it was evident on their faces. Think about it, Joseph had been falsely accused and wrongfully imprisoned, and yet Joseph noticed the sadness of these fellow prisoners' countenances and questioned them. In the natural, it seems Joseph would have been entitled to look sad, but he was not described this way. Even though Joseph had nothing outwardly to be happy about, he drew upon what he knew on the inside. The joy of the Lord was his strength.

The Bible does not indicate how long Joseph, the butler, and the baker were in prison together. More than likely, they did not know why Joseph was in prison but Joseph probably heard them discussing their situations. This particular morning, the reason they both looked sad was because of the dreams they had each dreamed the night before. Both men had had very vivid dreams and were troubled because they didn't understand what they meant. Joseph, "the dreamer," was gifted with interpreting dreams.

And they said to him, "We each have had a dream, and there is no interpreter of it." So Joseph said to them, "Do not interpretations belong to God? Tell them to me, please."

Genesis 40:8

Joseph Interprets

In the midst of his trial, Joseph was willing to minister to the butler and baker. It seemed Joseph would have been tempted to say to them, "You think you guys have had some dreams? You should hear about the dream God gave me eleven years ago!" But he did not. I can imagine a little voice whispering in Joseph's ear as he opened his mouth to interpret, "Really? You think you're going to interpret their dreams when your dream hasn't even come close to coming to pass! You really think you know how to interpret dreams?" Joseph unselfishly leaned upon the Spirit of God and was willing to interpret their dreams.

> *Then the chief butler told his dream to Joseph, and said to him, "Behold, in my dream a vine was before me, and in the vine were three branches; it was as though it budded, its blossoms shot forth, and its clusters brought forth ripe grapes. Then Pharaoh's cup was in my hand; and I took the grapes and pressed them into Pharaoh's cup, and placed the cup in Pharaoh's hand."*
>
> *Genesis 40:9-11*

After the chief butler shared his dream with Joseph, God gave Joseph the interpretation.

> *And Joseph said to him, "This is the interpretation of it: The three branches are three days. Now within three days Pharaoh will lift up your head and restore you to your place, and you will put Pharaoh's cup in his hand according to the former manner, when you were his butler."*
>
> *Genesis 40: 12-13*

Joseph interpreted the chief butler's dream and said, "You will be restored to your original position and it will happen within three days. The three branches on the vine represent three days."

> *But remember me when it is well with you, and please show kindness to me; make mention of me to Pharaoh, and get me out of this house. For indeed I was stolen away from the land of the Hebrews; and also I have done nothing here that they should put me into the dungeon.*
>
> *Genesis 40: 14-15*

Trust In God, Not In Man

Until this point in the story, Joseph had never tried to defend himself; but for the first time, Joseph was leaning on the arm of the flesh. In interpreting the chief butler's dream, Joseph realized this man could be his link to freedom. He was probably thinking, "This man will once again stand next to Pharaoh; in just three days he will be restored to his original position! Surely he will be so grateful for the interpretation of his dream that he will remember me and explain that I have been unjustly thrown in prison!"

Psalm 118:8-9 says, "*It is* better to trust in the LORD than to put confidence in man. *It is* better to trust in the LORD than to put confidence in princes."

When we are in need of deliverance from a situation, we have a tendency to think, "Maybe the owner of that company is my way of escape" or "Maybe if I had an opportunity to speak with the mayor, because of her connections, she could help make a way for my deliverance."

In this instance, Joseph was hoping the cupbearer would defend him. Notice again what Joseph said to the cupbearer, "And please remember me and do me a favor when things go well for you. Mention me to Pharaoh, so he might let me out of this place. For I was kidnapped from my homeland, the land of the Hebrews, and now I'm here in prison, but I did nothing to deserve it" (NLT, emphasis mine).

In the natural, it looks like God had forsaken Joseph, but in his heart Joseph knew He hadn't. However, Joseph allowed his emotions to be in control. He realized the cupbearer would be released and restored in three days. The number of "me's, I's, and my's" rapidly and freely flowed from Joseph's mouth. By leaning on the arm of the flesh, Joseph's release from prison was delayed by two years. The cupbearer completely forgot about him.

The Bible does not indicate how long it took for Joseph to repent of leaning on the arm of the flesh, placing his confidence in the ability of "princes" rather than God, but at some point he asked God to forgive him and he began to trust in God once again.

Jeremiah 17:5 says, "Cursed *is* the man who trusts in man and makes flesh his strength." When we put our trust in man, our heart has departed from the Lord. In other words, we remove our arm from God's and place it in the arm of man. It doesn't matter if we link arms with the president, vice-president, or the head of the FBI; when we remove our arm from God's, we have forsaken Him.

In hoping and trusting in a man, Joseph was forsaking God and opening himself up to a curse. His eyes, natural reasoning, and emotions told him, "These men can help get me out of this unfair situation." Joseph was trying to help the plan of God come to pass. I believe it was God's intention to use the cupbearer on Joseph's behalf, but Joseph just delayed the process by putting his trust in a man.

Jeremiah 17:5-8 says, "Thus says the LORD: 'Cursed *is* the man who trusts in man and makes flesh his strength, whose heart departs from the LORD. For he shall be like a shrub in the desert, and shall not see when good comes, but shall inhabit the parched places in the wilderness, *in* a salt land which is not inhabited. Blessed *is* the man who trusts in the LORD, and whose hope is the LORD. For he shall be like a tree planted by the waters, which spreads out its roots by the river, and will not fear when heat comes; but its leaf will be green, and will not be anxious in the year of drought, nor will cease from yielding fruit."

This passage is not referring to sinners, it is addressing believers whose hearts have departed from the Lord. Today there are many believers who are not trusting in God and instead have put their trust in man. They believe their deliverance is in knowing the right person, and they look to man. God is our deliverer!

Don't Be Like A Tumbleweed

The word "shrub" in verse 6, means "tumbleweed." Tumbleweeds are plants detached from a root system. They are blown here and there with no direction and nothing to stabilize them. We are like tumbleweeds when we put our trust in man instead of God. It is like having no root system, no stability, and the circumstances are blowing our lives wherever they can.

Verse 6 says when we put our faith in man rather than God, we "shall inhabit the parched places in the wilderness, in a salt land which is not inhabited." This means we are in a place where nothing in our lives can grow. But verses 7 and 8 say when we trust in the Lord and the Lord is our hope, our lives will be like thriving, fruitful trees. Wherever the water flows, trees live, even if the land all around is dead. When we trust in the Lord, everything around us may be dead, but because we are like trees planted by living waters, our lives will thrive. We are not dependent on circumstances; we are dependent on Jesus who is our flow of life!

Verse 8 promises, "For he shall be like a tree planted by the waters, which spreads out its roots by the river, and will not fear when heat (drought) comes; but its leaf will be green (continual prosperity), and will not be anxious (worried) in the year of drought, nor will cease from yielding fruit" (explanation mine).

Joseph had been in a barren place, but he prospered because his roots were planted in God. His trust was in God and not in man. However, in an emotional moment, Joseph turned to the cupbearer for help.

Interpretation Of The Chief Baker's Dream

When the chief baker saw that the interpretation was good, he said to Joseph, "I also was in my dream, and there were three white baskets on my head. In the uppermost basket were all kinds of baked goods for Pharaoh, and the birds ate them out of the basket on my head."

Genesis 40:16-17

The word "white" means "wicker" in this passage. The baker told Joseph he dreamt he had three wicker baskets on his head filled with baked goods, and birds were eating the baked goods.

> *So Joseph answered and said, "This is the interpretation of it: The three baskets are three days. Within three days Pharaoh will lift off your head from you and hang you on a tree; and the birds will eat your flesh from you."*
>
> *Genesis 40:18-19*

Joseph did not try to flatter the baker. He simply and honestly shared the interpretation God had given him. Joseph told the baker that in three days Pharaoh would sentence him to death and his flesh would be eaten by birds.

> *Now it came to pass on the third day, which was Pharaoh's birthday, that he made a feast for all his servants; and he lifted up the head of the chief butler and of the chief baker among his servants. Then he restored the chief butler to his butlership again, and he placed the cup in Pharaoh's hand. But he hanged the chief baker, as Joseph had interpreted to them.*
>
> *Genesis 40:20-22*

Joseph accurately interpreted both the butler's dream *and* the baker's dream. God had given him the interpretation.

Joseph Is Forgotten

> *Yet the chief butler did not remember Joseph, but forgot him.*
>
> *Genesis 40:24*

The chief butler did not remember what Joseph had shared with him. In fact, he completely forgot about Joseph. Joseph remained in prison for two more years. Joseph trusted man instead of God. He leaned on the arm of the flesh rather than on God. Only in trusting God will His plans come to pass in our lives.

How many times have we delayed the plan of God? How many times have we tried to help God bring His plan to pass in our lives? God's plan for Joseph had been delayed, but the good news is God is the redeemer of time. Sometimes we feel like we can't go any lower than the place of our current state. However, what God has spoken concerning His plan for our lives will come to pass. We must not lean on the arm of the flesh to bring it to pass. We must not give up. When we trust in God, His plan will come to pass!

Chapter 4

From The Pit To The Throne

We see mediocrity everywhere we look, mediocrity in government, mediocrity in business, mediocrity on the streets. It is all around us. Mediocre people seem to always disparage those who strive for excellence. This is what it was like between Joseph and his brothers. Ten of Joseph's eleven brothers were involved in every manner of mischief imaginable. They shirked their responsibilities, betrayed their brother, deceived their father, and the list goes on. Joseph's brothers resented him for being their father's favorite, but I believe they also resented him for being responsible, honest, trustworthy, mature, and the youngest of Jacob's sons.

Joseph continued to minister even though he was unjustly imprisoned. He became the lowest of prisoners and served both the butler and baker from Pharaoh's court who had been thrown in prison by Pharaoh. Just like Joseph, we are always ministers of the Lord regardless of what we are suffering in our own lives. A minister is not something we *do*; it is something we *are*. In the Christian life, sometimes we are on top of the heap, and sometimes the heap is on top of us! Regardless of whether things are going well in our lives or we are in a time of suffering, we must continue to minister into the lives of others.

Do Not Trust In Man

In Genesis 40, Joseph ministered to Pharaoh's chief butler and baker by accurately interpreting their dreams. The baker was sentenced to death, and the chief butler was restored to his former position in Pharaoh's court. Before the butler was released from prison, Joseph asked him to remember him when he was once again serving Pharaoh. Joseph made a mistake by putting his trust in man instead of God, and he remained in prison for two years. Genesis 40:23 says, "Yet the chief butler did not remember Joseph, but forgot him."

Pharaoh's Dreams

Pharaoh had a dream and in the dream, he was standing by the Nile River, one of the gods worshiped in Egypt.

> *Then it came to pass, at the end of two full years, that Pharaoh had a dream; and behold, he stood by the river. Suddenly there came up out of the river seven cows, fine looking and fat; and they fed in the meadow.*
>
> *Genesis 41:1-2*

In Pharaoh's dream, seven attractive, plump cows rose up out of the river. The Egyptians were very hygienic people. They were one of the few races, especially in the Middle East, who bathed once daily, and it was not uncommon for them to bathe twice in one day.

Not only did the Egyptians worship the Nile River, they also worshiped cows. In the Egyptian culture, these were two of the most worshipped gods because both provided life to the people.

*Then behold, seven other cows came up after them out of the
river, ugly and gaunt, and stood by the other cows on the bank
of the river. And the ugly and gaunt cows ate up the seven fine
looking and fat cows. So Pharaoh awoke.*

Genesis 41:3-4

Pharaoh was awakened by this first dream. What a dream!
From the Nile god that he worshiped arose seven healthy cows, gods
he also worshiped, which were eaten alive by seven ugly, starving
cows. Pharaoh was perplexed by the meaning of this dream but
fell asleep again.

*He slept and dreamed a second time; and suddenly seven heads
of grain came up on one stalk, plump and good. Then behold,
seven thin heads, blighted by the east wind, sprang up after
them. And the seven thin heads devoured the seven plump and
full heads. So Pharaoh awoke, and indeed, it was a dream.*

Genesis 41:5-7

The "east wind" mentioned in verse 6 was very hot and dry. In
the ancient world, especially in Egypt, it was called a *sirocco*. It was a
Mediterranean wind originating from the Sahara Desert that could
reach hurricane speeds. Whenever it arrived, crops would dry up.

This second dream caused Pharaoh to awaken again.

*Now it came to pass in the morning that his spirit was troubled,
and he sent and called for all the magicians of Egypt and all its
wise men. And Pharaoh told them his dreams, but there was
no one who could interpret them for Pharaoh.*

Genesis 41:8

These two dreams greatly troubled Pharaoh. In fact, they trouble Pharaoh so much he called for all of the magicians and wise men in Egypt to find the meaning of his dreams. He was searching for an interpretation, but not one of those he called could interpret his dreams. Pharaoh's dreams had been sent to him from God, but he had called for men who were sinners for the interpretation. It was impossible for them to interpret dreams that originated with God.

In 1 Corinthians 2:14, we are told, "But the natural man does not receive the things of the Spirit of God, for they are foolishness to him; nor can he know *them*, because they are spiritually discerned." None of Pharaoh's magicians or wise men could receive the things of the Spirit of God because those things are spiritually discerned.

Joseph Is Remembered

During this time, the cupbearer had been with Pharaoh. He listened as Pharaoh shared his dreams with all of the magicians and wise men of Egypt. He also witnessed the fact that there was no man in all of Pharaoh's entourage who could interpret his dreams. Then suddenly, after two years, he remembered Joseph. The cupbearer, who was responsible to memorize and remember the names of everyone he met so he could introduce them to Pharaoh when they wanted an audience with him, completely forgot about Joseph until this moment.

Then the chief butler spoke to Pharaoh, saying: "I remember my
faults this day. When Pharaoh was angry with his servants,
and put me in custody in the house of the captain of the guard,
both me and the chief baker, we each had a dream in one night,

*he and I. Each of us dreamed according to the interpretation
of his own dream. Now there was a young Hebrew man with
us there, a servant of the captain of the guard. And we told
him, and he interpreted our dreams for us; to each man he
interpreted according to his own dream. And it came to pass,
just as he interpreted for us, so it happened. He restored me to
my office, and he hanged him." Then Pharaoh sent and called
Joseph, and they brought him quickly out of the dungeon; and
he shaved, changed his clothing, and came to Pharaoh.*

Genesis 41:9-14

Joseph Prepares To Meet With Pharaoh

Pharaoh sent some guards to the prison to bring Joseph to
him. The Hebrew reading of this passage indicates the guards
had attempted to hastily bring Joseph before Pharaoh, but Joseph
wanted to shave and change his clothes before his meeting. After
two years in prison, Joseph probably looked unkempt and smelled
very "earthy." Imagine the guards rushing Joseph: "Move it! The
king wants you now! Hurry! You've got to interpret his dreams."

But Joseph knew the Egyptians were very clean people and
out of respect for their culture, he insisted on a shave and clean
clothes. "No. Bring me some clean clothes and a razor. Bring me
some water. Bring me some soap." This was another demonstration
of Joseph's integrity.

Pharaoh Seeks An Interpretation From Joseph

*And Pharaoh said to Joseph, "I have had a dream, and there
is no one who can interpret it. But I have heard it said of you
that you can understand a dream, to interpret it." So Joseph
answered Pharaoh, saying, "It is not in me; God will give
Pharaoh an answer of peace."*

Genesis 41:15-16

In verse 15, Pharaoh says, "I have heard that *you* can interpret
dreams." In verse 16, Joseph says, "It is not in me; only God can
interpret dreams!"

*Then Pharaoh said to Joseph: "Behold, in my dream I stood
on the bank of the river. Suddenly seven cows came up out of
the river, fine looking and fat; and they fed in the meadow.
Then behold, seven other cows came up after them, poor and
very ugly and gaunt, such ugliness as I have never seen in all
the land of Egypt. And the gaunt and ugly cows ate up the
first seven, the fat cows. When they had eaten them up, no one
would have known that they had eaten them, for they were
just as ugly as at the beginning. So I awoke. Also I saw in my
dream, and suddenly seven heads came up on one stalk, full and
good. Then behold, seven heads, withered, thin, and blighted
by the east wind, sprang up after them. And the thin heads
devoured the seven good heads. So I told this to the magicians,
but there was no one who could explain it to me. Then Joseph
said to Pharaoh, "The dreams of Pharaoh are one; God has
shown Pharaoh what He is about to do."*

Genesis 41:17-25

God gave Joseph the interpretation for both dreams. One

dream was addressing the meat of the kingdom and the other the agriculture of the kingdom. Although there were two dreams, the meaning was the same for both.

> *The seven good cows are seven years, and the seven good heads are seven years; the dreams are one. And the seven thin and ugly cows which came up after them are seven years, and the seven empty heads blighted by the east wind are seven years of famine. This is the thing which I have spoken to Pharaoh. God has shown Pharaoh what He is about to do. Indeed seven years of great plenty will come throughout all the land of Egypt; but after them seven years of famine will arise, and all the plenty will be forgotten in the land of Egypt; and the famine will deplete the land.*
>
> *Genesis 41:26-30*

Joseph explained that God was revealing to Pharaoh what was to come. First there would be seven years of prosperity. The crops would be plentiful and the land blessed. But that time of abundance would be followed by a great famine, and the abundance the land of Egypt once had would be quickly forgotten.

> *So the plenty will not be known in the land because of the famine following, for it will be very severe. And the dream was repeated to Pharaoh twice because the thing is established by God, and God will shortly bring it to pass.*
>
> *Genesis 41:31-32*

Joseph basically gave Pharaoh an explanation of his dreams stating that if the people were not wise and simply indulged themselves with the prosperity of the first seven years, those years would be devoured during the seven years that followed. Joseph also explained that the reason Pharaoh dreamed it twice was because God wanted to confirm to him that these events would surely come to pass, and they would come to pass quickly.

Joseph's Advice To Pharaoh

Now therefore, let Pharaoh select a discerning and wise man, and set him over the land of Egypt. Let Pharaoh do this, and let him appoint officers over the land, to collect one-fifth of the produce of the land of Egypt in the seven plentiful years. And let them gather all the food of those good years that are coming, and store up grain under the authority of Pharaoh, and let them keep food in the cities. Then that food shall be as a reserve for the land for the seven years of famine which shall be in the land of Egypt, that the land may not perish during the famine.

Genesis 41:33-36

The wisdom of God began to flow through Joseph and manifested as advice concerning Pharaoh's dreams and the impending famine. He suggested silos be built and twenty percent of the grain sown during the seven abundant years be stored in preparation for the seven years of drought. Joseph was in no way implying he was the wise man he was advising Pharaoh to find.

So the advice was good in the eyes of Pharaoh and in the eyes of all his servants. And Pharaoh said to his servants, "Can we find such a one as this, a man in whom is the Spirit of God?"

Genesis 41:37-38

From The Pit To The Throne

God's Spirit Recognized In Joseph

Joseph had been in prison for two years and during the previous thirteen years, he had been repeatedly treated unjustly. Standing before Pharaoh, at this moment, would have been a perfect time for Joseph to defend himself, to make a case about his innocence and the injustice of his current situation. Joseph was now thirty years old with nothing. In the natural, everything he ever had was gone. His clothes were "borrowed," and he used another man's razor to shave before being brought before Pharaoh. He was not married, had no children, and had lost the family he once belonged to. In every area of his life, Joseph had suffered loss, yet he continued to fulfill the will of God in his life! Even in his own testing, Joseph continued to reach out to help others. He provided an accurate interpretation of Pharaoh's dreams. The wisdom of God, through Joseph, revealed a plan for surviving the drought to come. When Joseph finished explaining what God had for him to share with Pharaoh, he stood, silently expecting to be escorted back to prison. Instead, Pharaoh unknowingly spoke out God's plan.

Then Pharaoh said to Joseph, "Inasmuch as God has shown you all this, there is no one as discerning and wise as you. You shall be over my house, and all my people shall be ruled according to your word; only in regard to the throne will I be greater than you." And Pharaoh said to Joseph, "See, I have set you over all the land of Egypt."

Genesis 41:39-41

Joseph stood before Pharaoh with nothing of his own, yet in nothing, he had everything. Pharaoh stood before Joseph, owning everything, and yet he had nothing because He had no understanding of the Creator of the universe! What is most important in life is not the abundance of things we own; it is Who we know! The things of this life can never buy eternal salvation, but eternal salvation can provide anything we need in this lifetime.

From Persecution To Promises Fulfilled

Prosperity never comes without testing — never. Position never comes without testing. Nothing we receive from God comes without testing. Matthew 10:30 says we can, "receive a hundredfold now in this time ... with persecutions." I believe the way we handle persecutions is how we will handle prosperity when it manifests.

For the past 13 years, Joseph had passed every test, with the exception of the time he asked the cupbearer to remember him in Pharaoh's presence. Because Joseph passed the many difficult tests in his life, the rewards would begin to manifest very, very quickly. Pharaoh placed Joseph in a position of great power in the nation of Egypt; only Pharaoh himself had more authority in the nation than Joseph!

Joseph is a type of the Lord Jesus Christ. In one split second of time, Jesus was raised from the pits of hell to sit at the right hand of God the Father. Joseph is also a type of us because when Jesus was raised from the dead, we were raised from the dead with Him! We were crucified and buried with Christ. We were laid in the grave with Him, but the same Spirit that raised Jesus from the dead lives in us and quickens our mortal bodies. We were raised from the dead and caused to sit at the right hand of the Father with Him! Joseph is a type of the Lord Jesus Christ, but He also is a type of us in salvation.

Second In Command

Then Pharaoh took his signet ring off his hand and put it on Joseph's hand; and he clothed him in garments of fine linen and put a gold chain around his neck. And he had him ride in the second chariot which he had; and they cried out before him, "Bow the knee!" So he set him over all the land of Egypt. Pharaoh also said to Joseph, "I am Pharaoh, and without your consent no man may lift his hand or foot in all the land of Egypt." And Pharaoh called Joseph's name Zaphnath-Paaneah. And he gave him as a wife Asenath, the daughter of Poti-Pherah priest of On. So Joseph went out over all the land of Egypt.

Genesis 41:42-45

Pharaoh removed his ring from his hand and placed it on Joseph's hand. The ring not only represented authority, it also represented power. Pharaoh's ring was a signet ring. It was used to legally stamp documents and considered equal to Pharaoh's own signature. In this one act, Pharaoh gave Joseph access to the treasuries and finances of Egypt. In addition, Joseph became the chief policymaker in all of Egypt, only second to Pharaoh himself!

Regardless of the circumstances surrounding Joseph, he always ended up second in command. Under his father, he was second in command over all of his brothers. After being sold into slavery, Potiphar made Joseph second in command over his household, only under Potiphar himself. He was thrown into prison and became second in command under the jailer who left the entire responsibility of overseeing the jail to Joseph. Now Pharaoh had made Joseph second in command over all of Egypt!

Pharaoh gave Joseph and Egyptian name, Zaphnath-paaneah, which means "interpreter of dreams and sustainer of life." He also gave Joseph a wife named Asenath who was the daughter of a man named Poti-pherah. Poti-pherah was the social leader of all the land of Egypt. Verse 45 says, "Joseph went out over all the land of Egypt," indicating his influence, literally, went throughout the entire land of Egypt.

Joseph Known Throughout The Land

Joseph was thirty years old when he stood before Pharaoh king of Egypt. And Joseph went out from the presence of Pharaoh, and went throughout all the land of Egypt.
Genesis 41:46

Prior to this one moment in time, Joseph was predominantly unknown in Pharaoh's kingdom. He was only known in prison and formerly known in Potiphar's household. However, because of Pharaoh's commission, Joseph suddenly became known throughout the land of Egypt. When the Egyptians heard the name of Joseph, they bowed, because he was second in command to Pharaoh.

Immeasurable Abundance

*Now in the seven plentiful years the ground brought forth
abundantly. So he gathered up all the food of the seven years
which were in the land of Egypt, and laid up the food in the
cities; he laid up in every city the food of the fields which
surrounded them. Joseph gathered very much grain, as the sand
of the sea, until he stopped counting, for it was immeasurable.*

Genesis 41:47-49

Initially, Joseph was calculating the amount of grain being
stored, but it became so abundant, he quit counting! Silos were
built and completely filled, and their crops were so abundant the
Egyptians were no longer able to keep track of it all!

*And to Joseph were born two sons before the years of famine
came, whom Asenath, the daughter of Poti-Pherah priest
of On, bore to him. Joseph called the name of the firstborn
Manasseh: "For God has made me forget all my toil and all
my father's house."*

Genesis 41:50-51

Joseph's two sons represented the half tribes of Manasseh and
Ephraim. Joseph named his first son Manasseh meaning "forgotten,"
signifying the past was over.

In Philippians 3:13-14 Paul said, "Brethren, I do not count
myself to have apprehended; but one thing I do, **forgetting** those
things which are behind and reaching forward to those things which
are ahead, I press toward the goal for the prize of the upward call
of God in Christ Jesus" (emphasis mine).

And the name of the second he called Ephraim: "For God has caused me to be fruitful in the land of my affliction."

Genesis 41:52

Ephraim means "fruitful" or "productive." The name of Joseph's second son symbolized Joseph's future. His first son he named for the past that was over and forgotten; the second son was named for the fruitfulness of the rest of Joseph's life.

Joseph chose to forget those things which were behind to reach forward to the prize of the high calling of God.

Then the seven years of plenty which were in the land of Egypt ended, and the seven years of famine began to come, as Joseph had said. The famine was in all lands, but in all the land of Egypt there was bread.

Genesis 41:53-54

The famine that came into the land not only affected Egypt, but it also affected the entire Middle East. One of the nations hit by this famine was Canaan, where Jacob was living.

So when all the land of Egypt was famished, the people cried to Pharaoh for bread. Then Pharaoh said to all the Egyptians, "Go to Joseph; whatever he says to you, do." The famine was over all the face of the earth, and Joseph opened all the storehouses and sold to the Egyptians. And the famine became severe in the land of Egypt. So all countries came to Joseph in Egypt to buy grain, because the famine was severe in all lands.

Genesis 41:55-57

A Witness Of God's Faithfulness

During the time of famine, Egypt made money. Throughout the Middle East, all countries came to Egypt to purchase grain, but when they came to Pharaoh for help, he sent them to see Joseph. God did not send the famine, and He did not cause the famine. He knew it was coming. God caused Joseph to be an evangelist, but instead of Joseph going to the people, God sent the people to him. Heathen nations suffered because of the famine, and they heard that Egypt had a supply of grain. They came to a man who knew God and could testify of His faithfulness. Satan intended for the famine to destroy lives, but God turned it right around and caused it to be a vehicle to spread the gospel of the Lord Jesus Christ.

What was Joseph doing while he was in prison? He was preaching. What did he do while he was in slavery? Preaching. What was he doing while he was alone with his brothers? Preaching. In good times and bad times, he testified about the God he served. Joseph's life serves as an example to us. Whether we're prospering or not prospering, we are still ministers. We minister in good times, bad times, up times, down times, in times, out times — it really doesn't matter. We are ministers for the Lord Jesus Christ in whatever circumstances we find ourselves. Like Joseph, if we keep our eyes fixed on the God who is forever faithful, we will see His promises to us come to pass no matter how impossible they seem.

Chapter 5

Reaping What You Sow

Hebrews 11:6 says of faith, "He who comes to God must believe that He is, and *that* He is a rewarder of those who diligently seek Him." There are some who do not believe God is a rewarder and instead, believe God hides Himself, destroys, and punishes mankind as part of His plan. However, God is a rewarder of those who diligently seek Him. God has predestined our rewards from the foundation of the world, and God let it be known in Joseph's life that he was headed toward a victory. Even though many years had passed since Joseph received the promise from God and though he was standing beside Pharaoh officiating the nation, he had still not seen God's promise come to pass in his life.

God can and does work through unbelievers to bring deliverance to our lives. God gave Pharaoh two dreams and through the interpretation of those dreams, God brought Joseph out of the prison into which he had been unjustly sentenced. God is not bound to working through believers alone. He worked through a donkey in the Old Testament, and He can certainly use an unbeliever!

The Blessing Of God

When the blessing of God manifested in Joseph's life, it remained until his death. Once Joseph walked into God's blessing, he never lost it. Tribulation always comes before greatness, and the way we handle tribulation indicates how we will handle greatness.

Joseph did not become joyful in his life because the circumstances surrounding him suddenly changed. He had joy long before being released from prison. Position wasn't the reason Joseph was blessed, although God used it as a blessing in his life. Money wasn't the reason he was blessed, although it was one of God's blessings. His family wasn't the reason Joseph was blessed, even though they were a blessing to his life. None of these things were the source of Joseph's joy. The Lord alone was the origin of his joy. Joseph was rewarded for the faithfulness he exhibited year after year, regardless of the circumstances in his life. He was faithful over the few things, and God made him ruler over much (Matthew 25:23).

Thirteen years had passed between the time Joseph was sold into slavery and his promotion by Pharaoh to be the second highest ruler over all of Egypt. After being promoted, the seven years of plenty had come, and yet Joseph stood twenty years past God's promise to him without seeing its fulfillment.

God had given Joseph a promise and regardless of whether it took the promise ten, twenty, or forty years to manifest, when God makes a promise, it is guaranteed to come to pass! Jesus promised He would one day return. Whether or not we see His return in our generation, He will return!

Twenty years had now passed in Joseph's life, and his family had not changed. Jacob was as self-centered as he had ever been. Joseph's brothers were still as carnal as they had been when they sold Joseph into slavery. By contrast, Joseph was a different man. He was now reigning over a nation. God had tremendously blessed him. Yet Joseph's family was still fighting with each other. Joseph had strength of character and deep dedication to the Lord. He never complained to others about his circumstances nor made excuses for himself. His brothers were constantly trying to obtain the top position, trying to gain recognition while diminishing the value of others.

It has been said that our candle never shines brighter by blowing out the candles of others; rather, if we light the candles around us, the light will greatly increase in the world! When we invest in the lives of others, God will be glorified. That is exactly how Joseph lived his life, regardless of the circumstances he encountered.

Jacob Sends His Sons To Egypt

When Jacob saw that there was grain in Egypt, Jacob said to his sons, "Why do you look at one another?" And he said, "Indeed I have heard that there is grain in Egypt; go down to that place and buy for us there, that we may live and not die." So Joseph's ten brothers went down to buy grain in Egypt. But Jacob did not send Joseph's brother Benjamin with his brothers, for he said, "Lest some calamity befall him."

Genesis 42:1-4

Jacob said to his sons, "Why are you standing around looking at each other wondering what to do during this famine? Go to Egypt! Get some grain so we don't starve to death!"

Benjamin had not been born at the time Joseph was sold into slavery by his brothers. Benjamin was the newcomer and the youngest in the family. Jacob would not allow Benjamin to travel with his brothers to Egypt. The memories of letting Joseph, his youngest son (at the time), out of his sight still haunted him. Joseph had been presumed dead. Verse 4 says, "But Jacob did not send Joseph's brother Benjamin with his brothers, for he said, 'Lest some calamity befall him.'"

And the sons of Israel went to buy grain among those who journeyed, for the famine was in the land of Canaan.

Genesis 42:5

When Jacob's older sons arrived in Egypt, they were just a few among thousands who had traveled to Egypt from every nation seeking grain. The process was slow. Every individual seeking to purchase grain was required to stand before one man — Joseph. People were thronging in the streets just waiting their turn to pass before him.

The Dream Revisited

Now Joseph was governor over the land; and it was he who

sold to all the people of the land. And Joseph's brothers came and bowed down before him with their faces to the earth.

Twenty years or more had passed since Joseph was sold into slavery by his brothers. Joseph never let go of God's promise to him. As his ten brothers were brought before Joseph, they did not recognize him. He was a boy when they sold him into slavery. Now, he was a man dressed as an Egyptian ruler. But he recognized them. Suddenly, they all bowed before Joseph just as he had witnessed in his dream so many years before, ten sheaves bowing down to the one that rose up and stood upright. The promise of God was coming to pass before his eyes!

Joseph saw his brothers and recognized them, but he acted as a stranger to them and spoke roughly to them. Then he said to them, "Where do you come from?" And they said, "From the land of Canaan to buy food."

Genesis 42:7

Even though Joseph recognized his brothers, he talked to them gruffly and in Egyptian through an interpreter (Genesis 42:23). Joseph could have spoken to them in Hebrew, but he did not want them to recognize him.

So Joseph recognized his brothers, but they did not recognize him. Then Joseph remembered the dreams which he had dreamed about them, and said to them "You are spies! You have come to see the nakedness of the land!"

Genesis 42:8-9

Joseph accused his brothers of being spies sent to search for the weaknesses in the defense of the Egyptian army in order to attack and steal grain rather than purchase it. He knew his accusations were false.

And they said to him, "No, my lord, but your servants have come to buy food. We are all one man's sons; we are honest men; your servants are not spies."

Genesis 42:10-11

Joseph's brothers responded, "We are honest men" and he knew this was absolutely untrue! Look at what they had done to him. Joseph kept accusing his brothers.

But he said to them, "No, but you have come to see the nakedness of the land."

Genesis 42:12

Joseph's Brothers Come Clean

And they said, "Your servants are twelve brothers, the sons of one man in the land of Canaan; and in fact, the youngest is with our father today, and one is no more."

Genesis 42:13

Their response to Joseph's accusation was true. They didn't claim that one of their brothers was dead but that he was "no more." Joseph suddenly realized, *Since I've been gone, there's been another son born! I have another brother!*

Reaping

But Joseph said to them, "It is as I spoke to you, saying 'You are
spies!' In this manner you shall be tested: By the life of Pharaoh,
you shall not leave this place unless your youngest brother
comes here. Send one of you, and let him bring your brother;
and you shall be kept in prison, that your words may be tested
to see whether there is any truth in you; or else, by the life of
Pharaoh, surely you are spies!" So he put them all together in
prison three days.

Genesis 42:14-17

Joseph had been unjustly thrown in the dungeon for two years.
Now his brothers were being unjustly thrown into prison for three
days. I believe, for twenty years, Joseph's brothers had never repented
for their sins. They were now reaping the consequence for what
they had sown in the past and never repented of.

Then Joseph said to them the third day, "Do this and live, for
I fear God: If you are honest men, let one of your brothers be
confined to your prison house; but you, go and carry grain for
the famine of your houses. And bring your youngest brother
to me; so your words will be verified, and you shall not die."
And they did so.

Genesis 42:18-20

I believe Joseph witnessed to everyone who had ever come
before him to purchase grain by saying, "I fear God." Joseph wasn't
afraid to tell others about his faith in God. In essence, Joseph said
to his brothers, "I know your God. I believe in your God."

In verse 19, Joseph challenges his brothers by saying, "If you are truly honest men as you claim, prove it to me. I will keep one of you in prison here in Egypt. The rest return home and bring your youngest brother back to Egypt with you."

> *Then they said to one another, "We are truly guilty concerning our brother, for we saw the anguish of his soul when he pleaded with us, and we would not hear; therefore this distress has come upon us." And Reuben answered them, saying "Did I not speak to you, saying, 'Do not sin against the boy'; and you would not listen? Therefore behold, his blood is now required of us."*
>
> *Genesis 42:21-22*

Joseph's brothers were speaking in Hebrew among themselves, not realizing Joseph could understand everything they were saying. Suddenly, because of being falsely accused, they remembered what they did to their brother, Joseph. They recalled the anguish in Joseph's voice as he cried out from the pit into which his brother placed him before selling him into slavery.

Reuben reminded his brothers in an accusatory tone, "I told you! I told you guys, 'Don't do this!' but you wouldn't listen to me! Now we are reaping the consequences of our actions!"

Reuben was noble but unstable. Many people have a desire to do what is right but choose not to. People may talk about doing what is right but then give in to pressure from others and don't follow through. Reuben knew killing Joseph, as he brothers desired to do, was wrong; but instead of standing up to them, he compromised. He suggested to his brothers that instead of killing Joseph, they lower him into a nearby pit, planning to later remove him and bring him back to his father. Reuben could have immediately rescued Joseph from his brothers but did not. The result of Reuben's inaction was Joseph being sold into slavery.

Reuben's Weakness

Genesis 49 records Jacob's prophesy over his sons. Verses 3 and 4 record Jacob's prophesy over Reuben.

Reuben, you are my firstborn, my might and the beginning of my strength, the excellency of dignity and the excellency of power. Unstable as water, you shall not excel, because you went up to your father's bed; then you defiled it — he went up to my couch.

Genesis 49:3-4

In verse 3, Jacob described Reuben as excelling in honor and power but continues in verse 4, describing him as unstable as water. Reuben possessed noble thoughts, but because of his instability, he did not act on those honorable ideas and thoughts and instead surrendered to outside pressure. Verse 4 also recounts a time when Reuben seduced his father's concubine, Bilhah, demonstrating Reuben's instability as he gave in to the pressure of lust rather than fleeing the temptation (Genesis 35:22).

Joseph understood everything his brothers were discussing as they finally admitted to one another that they had been completely heartless toward Joseph as he, in deep distress, pleaded with them not to sell him into slavery. Now they were reaping anguish in their souls for what they had sown into Joseph's life.

> *But they did not know that Joseph understood them, for he spoke to them through an interpreter. And he turned himself away from them and wept. Then he returned to them again, and talked with them. And he took Simeon from them and bound him before their eyes.*
>
> *Genesis 42:23-24*

Simeon Held And Imprisoned

Joseph then had Simeon bound before his brothers' eyes and had him sent to prison while sending all of the others back to Israel. Simeon would be held in prison until the brothers returned to Egypt with Benjamin.

> *Then Joseph gave a command to fill their sacks with grain, to restore every man's money to his sack, and to give them provisions for the journey. Thus he did for them. So they loaded their donkeys with the grain and departed from there. But as one of them opened his sack to give his donkey feed at the encampment, he saw his money; and there it was, in the mouth of his sack. So he said to his brothers, "My money has been restored, and there it is, in my sack!" Then their hearts failed them and they were afraid, saying to one another, "What is this that God has done to us?"*
>
> *Genesis 42:25-28*

Joseph's words and actions may have seemed cruel, but he was actually working a plan to bless his brothers and to reunite his entire family.

Joseph's brothers were carnal believers. Carnal Christians do not know how to handle the grace of God. They are so accustomed to the world's system, they believe they must work for anything they receive. Having their money returned to them caused Joseph's brothers to think the worst. In fact, "their hearts failed them and they were afraid." They didn't see God as being good and benevolent toward them. Instead, they thought God was out to punish them!

Then they went to Jacob their father in the land of Canaan and told him all that had happened to them, saying: "The man who is lord of the land spoke roughly to us, and took us for spies of the country. But we said to him, 'We are honest men; we are not spies. We are twelve brothers, sons of our father; one is no more, and the youngest is with our father this day in the land of Canaan.' Then the man, the lord of the country, said to us, 'By this I will know that you are honest men: Leave one of your brothers here with me, take food for the famine of your households, and be gone. And bring your youngest brother to me; so I shall know that you are not spies, but that you are honest men. I will grant your brother to you, and you may trade (move freely) in the land.'" Then it happened as they emptied their sacks, that surprisingly each man's bundle of money was in his sack; and when they and their father saw the bundles of money, they were afraid. (explanation mine)

Genesis 42:29-35

The one detail Joseph's brothers neglected to share with their father concerned the returned money one of the brothers found in his sack. Why did they withhold this information? They were *not* honest men.

Jacob's Grief

And Jacob their father said to them, "You have bereaved me: Joseph is no more, Simeon is no more, and you want to take Benjamin. All these things are against me."

Genesis 42:36

Jacob blamed his sons for his grief. He was totally focused on himself: "You have bereaved me. All these things are against me. Joseph's gone, Simeon's gone, and now you're telling me you want to take Benjamin away from me!"

All these many years after Joseph was sold into slavery, Jacob was still mourning his loss and had become bitter as a result. Jacob had never forgiven his sons. "It was your fault that Joseph disappeared. Now it's your fault Simeon is gone. And if I allow you to take Benjamin from me, he will probably never return, and it will be your fault!"

Jacob's Fear

Then Reuben spoke to his father, saying, "Kill my two sons if I do not bring him back to you; put him in my hands, and I will bring him back to you." But he said, "My son shall not go down with you, for his brother is dead, and he is left alone. If any calamity should befall him along the way in which you go, then you would bring down my gray hair with sorrow to the grave."

Genesis 42:37-38

Jacob was very pessimistic and basically complained, "I have been mourning over Joseph for twenty years and will mourn him until I go to the grave! Now Simeon is gone, and if I lose Benjamin too, I will die!"

In verse 37, Reuben's nobility and foolishness was exposed once again. He told Jacob, "Listen Dad. Let me take Benjamin back with me to Egypt, and if I do not return with him, I give you permission to kill both of my sons!" Reuben was trying to sound very noble, but how would Jacob killing Reuben's two sons have solved anything if Benjamin did not return? Reuben seemed to think this would pacify his father and lessen the impact of the loss if he failed to return with Benjamin. But Jacob still refused to allow his sons to return to Egypt while Simeon was waiting in prison, because of his fear of losing Benjamin.

> *Now the famine was severe in the land. And it came to pass, when they had eaten up the grain which they had brought from Egypt, that their father said to them, "Go back, buy us a little food." But Judah said to him, saying, "The man solemnly warned us, saying, 'You shall not see my face unless your brother is with you.' If you will send our brother with us, we will go down and buy you food. But if you will not send him, we will not go down, for the man said to us, 'You shall not see my face, unless your brother is with you.'"*
> *Genesis 43:1-5*

Only when the food his sons brought back from Egypt was depleted, did Jacob reluctantly allow his sons to return to Egypt. Jacob had learned to trust the Lord years before, but at this time, he was not speaking anything of faith. He was not declaring, "The Lord will preserve you. The Lord will keep you. The Lord will guide you." Jacob realized that unless he allowed Benjamin to go with his brothers to Egypt, he would never see them again.

Joseph's Character

The total opposite is found in Joseph's life. He continued to trust in the Lord, regardless of the circumstances surrounding him. Joseph was the type of believer who latched onto the character of God and blessed people, not based on *their* character, but based on the character Joseph possessed on the inside. He was a reflection of God. No matter what his brothers did to him, they could not destroy his character because Joseph's character was based on the unchanging character of God!

Chapter 6

The Return To Egypt

Now the famine was severe in the land. And it came to pass, when they had eaten up the grain which they had brought from Egypt, that their father said to them, "Go back, buy us a little food."

Genesis 43:1-2

Simeon was still being held in prison in Egypt and would not be released until his brothers returned with Benjamin, according to Joseph's demands. Joseph was testing his brothers and implemented three safeguards to ensure their return. First, Simeon was held in prison. Second, Joseph tested the honesty of the brothers by returning their money to them without their knowledge. Finally, Joseph demanded that Benjamin be brought to Egypt for Joseph to meet. The problem was that Jacob refused to allow the brothers to return to Egypt with Benjamin, even knowing Simeon was being held in prison. In fact, Jacob stated, "Simeon is no more," (Genesis 42:36) because he would not consent to the only plan that would bring him home.

Dominating Fear

Jacob's family was supposed to be the pinnacle of faith, but instead, they were filled with unbelief. They were descendants of Abraham, the father of our faith: Abraham, who put his faith in God and it was accounted to him for righteousness, and Abraham who learned to trust in the Lord.

Instead of being filled with faith, Jacob was filled with fear, and fear had been dominating his life for many years. In 1 John 4:18, we are told that fear has torment attached to it; because of the fear in his life, Jacob had been in torment since the loss of Joseph. Jacob allowed his God-given imagination to align itself with fear rather than with the promises of God, and he imagined the worst scenario concerning Benjamin.

There was a large contrast between Joseph and his father and brothers. Joseph's imagination was connected to his faith while Jacob and his sons linked their imaginations with fear. Joseph imagined the best; they imagined the worst.

Hunger Overrides Fear

After the food supplies had completely dwindled, verse 2 reveals that Jacob instructed his sons to return to Egypt for food.

Over the years, Jacob had shown partiality first toward Joseph and then toward Benjamin. If rain had fallen and crops had grown in Israel, no one would have returned to Egypt, even with the knowledge that Simeon was being held in prison. Jacob was afraid to lose the rest of his sons, especially Benjamin.

But Judah spoke to him, saying, "The man solemnly warned us, saying, 'You shall not see my face unless your brother is with you.' If you send our brother with us, we will go down and buy you food. But if you will not send him, we will not go down; for the man said to us, 'You shall not see my face unless your brother is with you.'"

Genesis 43:3-5

Judah reminded Jacob about the ultimatum he and his brothers were given by Joseph. Instead of thinking of the welfare of his family, Jacob thought only about himself.

Jacob's Self-Centeredness Revealed

And Israel (Jacob) said, "Why did you deal so wrongfully with me as to tell the man whether you had still another brother?" (explanation mine)

Genesis 43:6

Jacob basically whined, "Why did you do this to me? Why did you tell the man you had another brother?" His sons responded.

But they said, "The man asked us pointedly about ourselves and our family, saying, 'Is your father still alive? Have you another brother?' And we told him according to these words. Could we possibly have known that he would say, 'Bring your brother down'?"

Genesis 43:7

"Dad, we didn't offer the information. The man asked us very specific questions about you and our family. We had no idea he would ask us to bring Benjamin back to Egypt with us. It was totally unexpected!"

Then Judah said to Israel his father, "Send the lad with me, and we will arise and go, that we may live and not die, both we and you and also our little ones. I myself will be surety for him; from my hand you shall require him. If I do not bring him back to you and set him before you, then let me bear the blame forever. For if we had not lingered, surely by now we would have returned this second time."

Genesis 43:8-10

Judah continued, "Dad, I will personally guarantee Benjamin's safety, and if I don't bring him back, you can hold me responsible, and I will bear the blame forever. If we had not remained here all this time, we could have already gone back to Egypt and returned a second time. I really believe this man is a man of his word! He's probably wondering why we haven't yet returned for Simeon. The only reason you are allowing us to return at this time is not for Simeon, but for our own sake because we have no food."

Jacob's Pessimism And Lack Of Faith

And their father Israel said to them, "If it must be so, then do this: Take some of the best fruits of the land in your vessels and carry down a present for the man — a little balm and little honey, spices and myrrh, pistachio nuts and almonds. Take double money in your hand, and take back in your hand the money that was returned in the mouth of your sacks; perhaps it was an oversight. Take your brother also, and arise, go back to the man. And may God Almighty give you mercy before the man, that he may release your other brother and Benjamin. If I am bereaved, I am bereaved."

Genesis 43:11-14

Jacob's lack of faith is evident. Rather than trusting God for all of his sons to safely come back to him, including Simeon and Benjamin, instead of simply trusting that they would bring grain back with them from Egypt, Jacob tried to fix things. He returned double the money found in each of his sons' sacks along with gifts, hoping these would pacify Joseph and he would respond favorably toward his sons. Jacob was motivated by fear.

Jacob once again demonstrated his total lack of faith and said, "Hopefully the man in Egypt will show you mercy, release Simeon, and allow Benjamin to return, but if he doesn't and I never see any of you again, I will learn to live with my grief."

The Brothers Stand Before Joseph

So the men took that present and Benjamin, and they took double money in their hand, and arose and went down to Egypt; and they stood before Joseph. When Joseph saw Benjamin with them, he said to the steward of his house, "Take these men to my home, and slaughter an animal and make ready; for these men will dine with me at noon." Then the man did as Joseph ordered, and the man brought the men into Joseph's house.

Now the men were afraid because they were brought into Joseph's house; and they said, "It is because of the money, which was returned in our sacks the first time, that we are brought in, so that he may make a case against us and seize us, to take us as slaves with our donkeys."

Genesis 43:15-18

85

The brothers were frightened, and their imaginations were attached to fear. They imagined the very worst scenario. They believed Joseph was planning to make them slaves and confiscate their animals and all of their possessions because of the money found in their sacks when they returned home from Egypt after their first visit.

Joseph could have easily used this moment to avenge himself of the mistreatment he had suffered at the hands of his brothers. He stood in a position of authority and power and at his command could have had all of his brothers thrown into prison or put to death. But Joseph's character, integrity, and the presence of God in his life would not permit him to do so. His life was a representation of the life of Jesus Christ. Jesus was betrayed but remained faithful. Jesus was reviled but remained silent. Jesus consistently returned mercy and grace for the mistreatment and punishment He received from men. In fact, Jesus taught us in Matthew 5:11-12 (ESV), "Blessed are you when others revile you and persecute you and utter all kinds of evil against you falsely on my account. Rejoice and be glad, for your reward is great in heaven, for so they persecuted the prophets who were before you."

Joseph was not working for rewards on this earth; he was working for rewards in heaven. God stands behind any person who understands and extends the grace and mercy of God toward others.

When they drew near to the steward of Joseph's house, they talked with him at the door of the house, and said, "O sir, we indeed came down the first time to buy food; but it happened, when we came to the encampment, that we opened our sacks, and there, each man's money was in the mouth of his sack, our money in full weight; so we have brought it back in our hand. And we have brought down other money in our hands to buy food. We do not know who put our money in our sacks."

Genesis 43:19-22

The brothers now attempted to plead their case before Joseph's steward. They had anxiety about what Joseph was planning to do to them, and in fear, they attempt to build a case and defend themselves to Joseph's steward. Basically they told Joseph's steward, "We are innocent!"

Joseph Exhorts His Brothers To Trust God

But he said, "Peace be with you, do not be afraid. Your God and the God of your father has given you treasure in your sacks; I had your money." Then he brought Simeon out to them.

Genesis 43:23

It is interesting to note, the brothers are being witnessed to by an Egyptian who is telling them to trust in their God and the God of their father! I believe this indicates that Joseph had witnessed to his entire Egyptian household. I believe this steward became a believer because of Joseph's witness, and now he was encouraging Joseph's brothers to trust in *their* God and the God of *their* father! He was not afraid to witness!

So the man brought the men into Joseph's house and gave them water, and they washed their feet; and he gave their donkeys feed. Then they made the present ready for Joseph's coming at noon, for they heard that they would eat bread there.

Genesis 43:24-25

Not only did the steward bring the brothers into Joseph's house, give them water, and wash their feet, he also fed their donkeys!

And when Joseph came home, they brought him the present which was in their hand into the house, and bowed down before him to the earth. Then he asked them about their well-being, and said, "Is your father well, the old man of whom you spoke? Is he still alive?" And they answered "Your servant our father is in good health; he is still alive." And they bowed their heads down and prostrated themselves.

Genesis 43:26-28

Joseph's Dream Unfolds

For a second time, Joseph's dream came to pass as his brothers bowed their heads and prostrated themselves before Joseph.

Then he lifted his eyes and saw his brother Benjamin, his mother's son, and said, "Is this your younger brother of whom you spoke to me?" And he said "God be gracious to you, my son." Now his heart yearned for his brother; so Joseph made haste and sought somewhere to weep. And he went into his chamber and wept there.

Genesis 43:29-30

Joseph had never met his brother, Benjamin. Seeing him for the first time, Joseph was completely overcome with emotion, ran to his bedroom, and wept. He didn't want to weep in the presence of his brothers; he wasn't ready to reveal himself to them.

Then he washed his face and came out; and he restrained himself, and said, "Serve the bread." So they set him a place by himself, and them by themselves, and the Egyptians who ate with him by themselves; because the Egyptians could not eat food with the Hebrews, for that is an abomination to the Egyptians. And they sat before him, the firstborn according to his birthright and the youngest according to his youth; and the men looked in astonishment at one another.

Genesis 43:31-33

Imagine this scene. The Egyptians were sitting in one place, and the house workers sat in another place. Joseph sat with his brothers. It was an abomination to the Egyptians for them to mingle with the Hebrews. Joseph's brothers were probably looking at one another wondering why this powerful Egyptian was seated with them.

Then he took servings to them from before him, but Benjamin's serving was five times as much as any of theirs. So they drank and were merry with him.

Genesis 43:34

The brothers now realized Joseph did not intend to harm them. Simeon had been released, and they observed how Joseph treated Benjamin. They saw God's love and mercy being displayed through Joseph but still had no inkling that they were sitting in the presence of their brother. Benjamin's serving was five times greater than what his brothers received. In the Bible, five is the number for God's grace.

Joseph Instructs His Steward

And he commanded the steward of his house, saying, "Fill the men's sacks with food, as much as they can carry, and put each man's money in the mouth of his sack. Also put my cup, the silver cup, in the mouth of the sack of the youngest, and his grain money. So he did according to the word that Joseph had spoken.

Genesis 44:1-2

Joseph instructed his steward to return the money his brothers had brought with them to Egypt, which was double the amount they had originally brought to pay for the first sack of grain plus the amount for the second sack they came for because of the continued drought in the land.

Joseph had time to observe the integrity of his brothers' hearts by returning their money plus another bag of money to test their honesty; he had also observed the fact that they never returned for Simeon until this moment, revealing their motive: they needed food! Knowing his brothers had not returned for Simeon or even to restore the money from their first trip, Joseph still extended God's grace toward them. Every time Joseph was "squeezed" in his life, vengeance didn't spew out; instead, God's mercy and grace were released toward others.

In addition to returning their money, Joseph also instructed his steward to place his silver cup in the mouth of Benjamin's sack. This cup was part of the Egyptian culture and was called a "divining cup." It was used by Egyptians for decision making and was associated with Egyptian gods. Even though Joseph owned a divining cup, it held no power and was meaningless to him. He knew there was no power in the cup.

Some Christians are fearful of allowing certain emblems in their homes, frightened these will somehow jump off the shelf and cause certain havoc. There was a time when owls were popular, but in some Christian circles they were considered evil and if you had statues, pictures, or anything with an owl in your home, people would say, "You know, they have an owl in their home. That is an evil symbol." But God created owls! If a family fell down and worshiped that owl every day at noon, I would think something is wrong; it is possible for demons to be attached to objects that are worshiped by men and women. But if an owl is simply part of their décor, there is absolutely nothing wrong with it! I am not suggesting that believers set up statues or hang paintings of Buddha in their homes; but neither should we expect demons to be running around coming from inanimate objects that are neither good nor evil.

The silver divining cup Joseph asked to be placed in Benjamin's sack was, however, very valuable.

As soon as the morning dawned, the men were sent away, they and their donkeys. When they had gone out of the city, and were not yet far off, Joseph said to his steward, "Get up, follow the men; and when you overtake them, say to them, 'Why have you repaid evil for good? Is not this the one from which my lord drinks, and with which he indeed practices divination? You have done evil in so doing.'"

Genesis 44:3-5

Joseph wanted to ensure that his family would return, including his father. He knew the way to do that was to have a reason for them to return.

Joseph's Silver Cup "Discovered"

So he overtook them, and he spoke to them these same words. And they said to him, "Why does my lord say these words? Far be it from us that your servants should do such a thing. Look, we brought back to you from the land of Canaan the money which we found in the mouth of our sacks. How then could we steal silver or gold from your lord's house? With whomever of your servants it is found, let him die, and we also will be my lord's slaves."

Genesis 44:6-9

The steward obeyed Joseph and repeated what Joseph instructed him to say to his brothers. The brothers were so certain none of them would have stolen from Joseph, they told the steward, "We don't know how you could accuse us of such a thing. Why would we steal from your master? We returned the money that we found in our sacks after the first trip. None of us would steal from your master! In fact, if you find the cup in any of our sacks, kill the one who stole it, and the rest of us will be your slaves."

And he said, "Now also let it be according to your words; he with whom it is found shall be my slave, and you shall be blameless."

Genesis 44:10

Joseph's steward said, "I will do what you say, but instead of killing the man who has stolen and making the others slaves, only the guilty brother will be made a slave; the rest may go free."

Then each man speedily let down his sack to the ground, and each opened his sack. So he searched. He began with the oldest and left off with the youngest; and the cup was found in Benjamin's sack. Then they tore their clothes, and each man loaded his donkey and returned to the city.

Genesis 44:11-13

As Joseph had orchestrated, the steward searched every man's bag, beginning with the eldest brother and ending with the youngest. To the shock of all of the brothers, the steward found the cup in Benjamin's bag.

So Judah and his brothers came to Joseph's house, and he was still there; and they fell before him on the ground. And Joseph said to them, "What deed is this you have done? Did you not know that such a man as I can certainly practice divination?" Then Judah said, "What shall we say to my lord? What shall we speak? Or how shall we clear ourselves? God has found out the iniquity of your servants; here we are, my lord's slaves, both we and he also with whom the cup was found." But he said, "Far be it from me that I should do so; the man in whose hand the cup was found, he shall be my slave. And as for you, go up in peace to your father."

Genesis 44:14-17

Judah Pleads His Case

After the cup was found in Benjamin's bag, the brothers returned to Joseph's house to make an appeal on Benjamin's behalf. They fell to the ground before Joseph offering to become his slaves, but Joseph released them to return to their father. He had pre-determined to keep Benjamin alone as his slave.

Then Judah came near to him and said: "O my lord, please let your servant speak a word in my lord's hearing, and do not let your anger burn against your servant; for you are even like Pharaoh. My lord asked his servants, saying, 'Have you a father or a brother?' And we said to my lord, 'We have a father, an old man, and a child of his old age, who is young; his brother is dead, and he alone is left of his mother's children, and his father loves him.' Then you said to your servants, 'Bring him down to me, that I may set my eyes on him.' And we said to my lord, 'The lad cannot leave his father, for if he should leave his father, his father would die.' But you said to your servants, 'Unless your youngest brother comes down with you, you shall see my face no more.' So it was, when we went up to your servant my father, that we told him the words of my lord. And our father said, 'Go back and buy us a little food.' But we said, 'We cannot go down; if our youngest brother is with us, then we will go down; for we may not see the man's face unless our youngest brother is with us.' Then your servant my father said to us, 'You know that my wife bore me two sons; and the one went out from me, and I said, "Surely he is torn to pieces"; and I have not seen him since. But if you take this one also from me, and calamity befalls him, you shall bring down my gray hair with sorrow to the grave.' Now therefore, when I come to your servant my father, and the lad is not with us, since his life is bound up in the lad's life, it will happen, when he sees that the lad is not with us, that he will die. So your servants will bring down the gray hair of your servant our father with sorrow to the grave. For your servant became surety for the lad to my father, saying, 'If I do not bring him back to you, then I shall bear the blame before my father forever.' Now therefore, please let your servant remain instead of the lad as a slave to my lord, and let the lad go up with his brothers. For how shall I go up to my father if the lad is not with me, lest perhaps I see the evil that would come upon my father?"

Genesis 44:18-34

In despair at the thought of returning to Canaan without Benjamin, Judah began to share with Joseph genuinely and sincerely from his heart. He explained how Jacob had had two sons by the same wife and how one of his sons was assumed to be torn to pieces by a wild animal. He described how his father had already lost one son, and if they returned to their father without Benjamin, it would literally bring about the death of their father!

In spite of how Joseph's brothers had treated him in the past, once again, Joseph would allow the love, mercy, and grace of the Lord Jesus Christ to flow through him toward his brothers.

Chapter 7

The Blessing Overflowing

Psalm 105 is a song about the history of the children of Israel.

Moreover He called for a famine in the land; He destroyed all the provision of bread. He sent a man before them — Joseph — who was sold as a slave. They hurt his feet with fetters, he was laid in irons. Until the time that his word came to pass, the word of the LORD tested him. The king sent and released him, the ruler of the people let him go free. He made him lord of his house, and ruler of all his possessions, to bind his princes at his pleasure, and teach his elders wisdom. Israel also came into Egypt, and Jacob dwelt in the land of Ham. He increased His people greatly, and made them stronger than their enemies.

Psalm 105:16-24

Joseph's Dream Comes To Pass At Last

The *Amplified Classic* version of verses 18 and 19 say of Joseph, "His feet they hurt with fetters; he was laid in chains of iron *and* his soul entered into the iron, until his word [to his cruel brothers] came true, until the word of the Lord tried *and* tested him." God had given Joseph His word long before the time Joseph entered Egypt. God's word had come to Joseph in the form of a dream. Through that dream, God ministered to Joseph that a day would come when his brothers would bow down to him; in fact, an entire nation would bow down to him. This word, given so many years before, had now come to pass.

Although the famine came, as God had revealed through Pharaoh's dream, God had a plan of deliverance for both Joseph and the entire land of Israel.

Judah had made his case before Joseph about surrendering himself to Joseph to be his slave instead of Benjamin. Judah demonstrated selflessness and true concern about the welfare of his father and youngest brother. Joseph was overcome with emotion in seeing his brothers response, yet he still had not revealed his true identity to his brothers.

Joseph Reveals Himself To His Brothers

Then Joseph could not restrain himself before all those who stood by him, and he cried out, "Make everyone go out from me!" So no one stood with him while Joseph made himself known to his brothers. And he wept aloud, and the Egyptians and the house of Pharaoh heard it. Then Joseph said to his brothers, "I am Joseph; does my father still live?" But his brothers could not answer him, for they were dismayed in his presence.

Genesis 45:1-3

Joseph cried out so loudly, everyone in Pharaoh's house heard his cry. The word "dismayed" means they were terrified in his presence. Suddenly, they understood they had been in the presence of Joseph, the brother they had betrayed so many years before!

The Blessing Overflowing

Sent To Preserve Life

And Joseph said to his brothers, "Please come near to me." So they came near. Then he said: "I am Joseph your brother, whom you sold into Egypt. But now, do not therefore be grieved or angry with yourselves because you sold me here; for God sent me before you to preserve life.

Genesis 45:4-5

Notice how Joseph responded to his brothers, "God sent me before you to preserve life." In verse 7 he says, "God sent me before you to preserve a posterity for you," in verse 8, "it was not you who sent me here, but God."

The nobility of Joseph's character rose up despite all the persecution he had experienced while the Word of the Lord "tried and tested him." In addition, Satan tried to destroy and discourage him so he would abandon the dream God had placed in his heart. Yet in everything, Joseph kept the proper perspective, looking past it all to recognize the hand of the Lord upon his life.

It is important to understand it was not God's will for Joseph's brothers to sell him into slavery. God had a plan to deliver Joseph from man's plans against him, to rescue him from Satan's schemes to destroy him. Proverbs 26:27 says, "Whoever digs a pit will fall into it, and he who rolls a stone will have it roll back on him."

Picture walking innocently down a hill as someone climbs to the top of the hill intending to roll a mammoth bolder down the hill toward you. However, about the time they climb to the top of the hill, their feet slip and the boulder rolls back over them instead.

The point is God sees everything! Man can be conniving and making plans against us without our knowledge, but they cannot hide from God. Circumstances may take us by surprise, but they never take God by surprise.

When Joseph's brothers sold him into slavery, God had a plan for him in Egypt. When Pharaoh's wife falsely accused Joseph and he was unjustly thrown into prison, God had a plan for him in prison. When his time in prison was prolonged due to the neglect of others, God had a plan there too!

Through all of these setbacks, Joseph was exalted to one of the highest positions in Egypt, just below Pharaoh himself. God blessed Potiphar's house for Joseph's sake, God blessed the prison for Joseph's sake, and now God blessed the entire nation of Egypt for Joseph's sake.

Regardless of where we are in life, God can bless others because of our presence — because of His presence in us! God can turn an entire family around because of the presence of one believer! The Bible teaches us that a sanctified wife married to an unbeliever can sanctify an entire household because of her presence; a sanctified husband married to an unbeliever can sanctify and entire household because of his presence. One believer in a home with unbelievers can give God an inroad into that family to bless them.

The same was true of Joseph's presence wherever he was. Whether it was the nation of Egypt, Joseph's family, or the nation of Israel, all were blessed because of Joseph's presence. Through everything that had come against Joseph, he always kept his eyes on the Lord.

The Blessing Overflowing

"For these two years the famine has been in the land, and there are still five years in which there will be neither plowing nor harvesting. And God sent me before you to preserve a posterity for you in the earth, and to save your lives by a great deliverance."

Genesis 45:6-7

Joseph's brothers sold him into slavery and were indifferent to the fact that he might have lost his life after they sold him. Now Joseph was saving their lives. He treated them with grace. Grace is never deserved or earned. Joseph's brothers should have reaped what they sowed, but instead, Joseph displayed the character of the Lord Jesus Christ toward them. "Love your enemies" (Matthew 5:44). "Do good to those who hate you, bless those who curse you, pray for those who spitefully use you" (Luke 6:28). "Be merciful, just as your Father also is merciful" (Luke 6:36).

So now it was not you who sent me here, but God; and He has made me a father to Pharaoh, and lord of all his house, and a ruler throughout all the land of Egypt.

Genesis 45:8

Literally, Joseph said to his brothers, "God made me a father under Pharaoh, not only over his entire household, but over the entire nation under him."

400 Years In Egypt Revealed To Abraham

Genesis 15 recounts the Abrahamic covenant. God spoke to Abram and explained how the nation of Israel would come from his loins. He also revealed the future of that nation, that they would be slaves in Egypt until their ultimate deliverance.

> *Then He said to Abram: "Know certainly that your descendants will be strangers in a land that is not theirs, and will serve them, and they will afflict them four hundred years. And also the nation whom they serve I will judge; afterward they shall come out with great possessions.*
>
> *Genesis 15:13-14*

God was making reference to the specific time when Israel would be in the land of Egypt. God would open the way for Israel to enter the land of Egypt when Satan was attacking the land. God did not send the famine to Israel or Egypt; Satan did. Why? Satan has always been out to destroy the nation of Israel because of the promise, found in Genesis 3:15: "And I will put enmity between you (Satan) and the woman, and between your seed (Satan's) and her Seed (Jesus Christ); He (Jesus Christ) shall bruise your (Satan's) head, and you (Satan) shall bruise His (Jesus Christ's) heel" (explanations mine).

Satan's Attempts To Destroy "The Seed"

Because of this promise, Satan has tracked the seed of the woman throughout the ages. Satan does not value life and goes to extremes to destroy lives, especially the lives of God's chosen people. After the time of Joseph, the population of Israel greatly increased, and the king of Egypt, being threatened by their numbers, commanded all of the midwives to kill any male child born in Israel. These women feared God, so they did not follow his command, and the population of Israel continued to increase. Finally, Pharaoh commanded that any male child born in Israel to be thrown into the Nile River. This was the time in which Moses was born. During the time of Jesus' birth, Herod gave orders for all of the male children born who were two years old or younger to be killed in an attempt to destroy the Savior.

Satan has persisted in his attempt to destroy the Seed of the woman, which included Abraham, Isaac, Jacob, and Jacob's twelve sons: ultimately, the nation of Israel. At the time Jacob, his twelve sons, and their families entered Egypt, Israel was comprised of seventy-five people. Satan sent a famine to Egypt and the entire Middle East just to destroy seventy-five people!

Proper Perspective In Times Of Adversity

Joseph became a type of savior to preserve the posterity of God's people. While famine entered the land of Egypt and extended throughout the land of Israel, God raised up Joseph to save His people; for 400 years, the children of Israel would remain in the land of Egypt. Adversity would eventually come against them, but Israel would increase from a nation of seventy-five to over two million when they left the bondage of Egypt, led by Moses 400 years later.

Joseph is an example of becoming stronger under pressure and during times of adversity. He came through every trial and emerged stronger than he was before. Why? Because he kept his focus on the Lord; he kept his eyes on the promises of God. It is not the troubles and trials that make us stronger, however. If this were the case, every Christian would be strong because we all face troubles and trials. It is perspective during difficult times, the shield of faith, the sword of the Spirit, the armor of God, His Word put into practice, and keeping our eyes on Him that makes us stronger.

God was not taken by surprise when Joseph was sold by his brothers, falsely accused by Potiphar's wife, thrown into prison, or forgotten by Pharaoh's cupbearer. There is nothing we can walk into in our lives that God doesn't already know about; He already has a plan for deliverance. We simply need to look to Him, to seek Him for His plan. God used Joseph at this time to cause the nation of Israel to become stronger and greater than ever before.

Joseph's Message To His Father

Hurry and go up to my father, and say to him, "Thus says your son Joseph: 'God has made me lord of all Egypt; come down to me, do not tarry. You shall dwell in the land of Goshen, and you shall be near to me, you and your children, your children's children, your flocks and your herds, and all that you have. There I will provide for you, lest you and your household, and all that you have, come to poverty; for there are still five years of famine.'"

Genesis 45:9-11

In verse 10, Joseph sent a message to his father saying, "You shall dwell in the land of Goshen." Joseph had already prepared a piece of property for his family with Pharaoh's approval. God continued to bless the land of Goshen for the sake of Israel until they were finally delivered by Moses.

"And behold, your eyes and the eyes of my brother Benjamin see that it is my mouth that speaks to you. So you shall tell my

*father of all my glory in Egypt, and of all that you have seen;
and you shall hurry and bring my father down here." Then he
fell on his brother Benjamin's neck and wept, and Benjamin
wept on his neck. Moreover he kissed all his brothers and wept
over them, and after that his brothers talked with him.*

Genesis 45:12-15

Once again Joseph's character was revealed in his forgiving,
loving, and gracious attitude toward his brothers.

God's Grace Extended

*Now the report of it was heard in Pharaoh's house, saying,
"Joseph's brothers have come." So it pleased Pharaoh and
his servants well. And Pharaoh said to Joseph, "Say to your
brothers, 'Do this: Load your animals and depart; go to the land
of Canaan. Bring your father and your households and come to
me; I will give you the best of the land of Egypt, and you will
eat the fat of the land. Now you are commanded — do this:
Take carts out of the land of Egypt for your little ones and your
wives; bring your father and come. Also do not be concerned
about your goods, for the best of all the land of Egypt is yours.'"*

Genesis 45:16-20

When Pharaoh heard about Joseph's brothers, he was pleased
and told Joseph to instruct his brothers to load their animals, go
back to Israel, and bring back their father and households. He also
promised that Joseph's family would be given the very best of the
land of Egypt and would never lack anything in their lives. They
would have the best homes in the land and eat the best food in all
of Egypt.

I can just imagine Joseph's brothers looking at each other and thinking, *We have been scoundrels. We have been unkind. We have maligned. We have used. We have sold our brother into slavery, and look what God did for him — our brother whose dreams we mocked and ridiculed. We came to buy some grain, and we have been blessed with abundance!*

Joseph's brothers were so accustomed to trying to get ahead by their own devices, stepping on people, abusing people, and manipulating circumstances to their own advantage, that they never received of God's grace. In the past, Joseph made them angry just because he believed the dream God had given him was a promise that would come to pass. When they sold him into slavery, they thought they had rid themselves of Joseph. Legalism hates grace, and Joseph represented the grace and blessing of God. Selling Joseph didn't remove God's blessing on Joseph's life. That grace caused Joseph to be a blessing and prosper, regardless of where he found himself!

Joseph maintained his love for his brothers - even after all the adversity he had experienced that was put into motion by their actions - and he began pouring out undeserved blessings on them. This is a type of the Lord Jesus Christ. It doesn't matter how many times we have blamed Him, cursed Him, turned our backs on Him, He will not remove His grace from us because grace is never dependent on us; it is dependent on Him. God gives because of His character, not because of our character. God never fails! Joseph was a type of Him.

When we begin to follow after the Lord and we begin to follow after His Word and we begin to live out the Christian life every day, the character of God becomes manifest through our lives and we start acting in more grace toward people than we ever thought possible because we live out the character of Christ in our own life. This is what happed with Joseph.

In verse 20, Joseph told his brothers, "Once you are back in Israel and prepare to return to Egypt, don't worry about your possessions, because you will have the best of whatever you want or need available to you when you settle in Egypt."

Pharaoh basically said, "I've got everything you will ever need. Anything you want to move here is fine, but anything you don't want to move, you will find something even better when you get here."

Abundance For The Trip

Then the sons of Israel did so; and Joseph gave them carts, according to the command of Pharaoh, and he gave them provisions for the journey. He gave to all them, to each man, changes of garments; but to Benjamin he gave three hundred pieces of silver and five changes of garments. And he sent to his father these things: ten donkeys loaded with good things of Egypt, and ten female donkeys loaded with grain, bread, and food for his father for the journey. So he sent his brothers away, and they departed; and he said to them, "See that you do not become troubled along the way."

Genesis 45:21-24

According to the command of Pharaoh, Joseph sent his brothers back to Israel with an abundance of food that would last them until they arrived home and returned again to Egypt with their father.

Jacob's Response To News Of Joseph

Then they went up out of Egypt, and came to the land of
Canaan to Jacob their father. And they told him, saying "Joseph
is still alive, and he is governor over all the land of Egypt."
And Jacob's heart stood still, because he did not believe them.
But when they told him all the words which Joseph had said
to them, and when he saw the carts which Joseph had sent to
carry him, the spirit of Jacob their father revived. Then Israel
said, "It is enough. Joseph my son is still alive. I will go and see
him before I die."

Genesis 45:25-28

Jacob's heart literally stopped beating for a moment, and he
became faint because of the shocking news that Joseph was alive.
Initially, he did not believe what his sons were telling him, but when
they shared what Joseph had spoken to them and he saw the wagons
Joseph had sent, Jacob was revived. Jacob made plans to travel to
Egypt with his sons to be reunited with Joseph.

Jacob At Beersheba

So Israel took his journey with all that he had, and came to
Beersheba, and offered sacrifices to the God of his father Isaac.

Genesis 46:1

Abraham mentioned Beersheba in Genesis 21:31. *Beersheba*
means "the well of the oath." It was the place where Jacob had

entered into a covenant relationship with God. Now Jacob came to Beersheba and "offered sacrifices to the God of his father Isaac," but why had he waited to worship God until *after* he learned Joseph was alive? He could have been worshiping God all those years, but instead, he believed the evidence presented to him that Joseph was dead. By faith, Jacob should have made a practice of traveling to Beersheba and offering sacrifices to the Lord for the deliverance of his children. Instead, he was controlled by the fear of losing them. He even accepted leaving Simeon in jail as a slave in Egypt because he was afraid he would lose his other sons if he allowed them to return to Egypt for Simeon. And he certainly would not allow Benjamin to travel to Egypt. Jacob lived his life continually in fear. Only when he realized the circumstances had changed did he choose to worship the Lord! He was not living by faith.

> *Then God spoke to Israel in the visions of the night, and said, "Jacob, Jacob!" And he said, "Here I am." So He said, "I am God, the God of your father; do not fear to go down to Egypt, for I will make of you a great nation there. I will go down with you to Egypt, and I will also surely bring you up again; and Joseph will put his hand on your eyes."*
>
> *Genesis 46:2-4*

God addressed Jacob's fear. In this instance, he was afraid to go to Egypt. God assured Jacob He would go with him. When God told Jacob, "Joseph will put his hand on your eyes," the literal meaning was Jacob would die in Egypt, but Joseph would be the one to close his eyes after his death.

Then Jacob arose from Beersheba; and the sons of Israel carried their father Jacob, their little ones, and their wives, in the carts which Pharaoh had sent to carry him. So they took their livestock and their goods, which they had acquired in the land of Canaan, and went to Egypt, Jacob and all his descendants with him. His sons and his sons' sons, his daughters, and all his descendants he brought with him to Egypt.

Genesis 46:5-7

Jacob's sons carried him along with their wives and little children in the wagons Joseph had provided. They also brought along their personal possessions and livestock with them as they made the trek to Egypt.

Jacob's Descendants

The next passage lists Jacob's descendants.

Now these were the names of the children of Israel, Jacob and his sons, who went to Egypt: Reuben was Jacob's firstborn. The sons of Reuben were Hanoch, Pallu, Hezron, and Carmi. The sons of Simeon were Jemuel, Jamin, Ohad, Jachin, Zohar, and Shaul, the son of a Canaanite woman. The sons of Levi were Gershon, Kohath, and Merari. The sons of Judah were Er, Onan, Shelah, Perez, and Zerah (but Er and Onan died in the land of Canaan). The sons of Perez were Hezron and Hamul. The sons of Issachar were Tola, Puvah, Job, and Shimron. The sons of Zebulun were Sered, Elon, and Jahleel. These were the sons of Leah, whom she bore to Jacob in Padan Aram, with his daughter Dinah. All the persons, his sons and his daughters, were thirty-three. The sons of Gad were Ziphion Haggi,

Shuni, Ezbon, Eri, Arodi, and Areli. The sons of Asher were Jimnah, Ishuah, Isui, Beriah, and Serah, their sister. And the sons of Beriah were Heber and Malchiel. These were the sons of Zilpah, whom Laban gave to Leah his daughter; and these she bore to Jacob: sixteen persons. The sons of Rachel, Jacob's wife, were Joseph and Benjamin. And to Joseph in the land of Egypt were born Manasseh and Ephraim, whom Asenath, the daughter of Poti-Pherah priest of On, bore to him. The sons of Benjamin were Belah, Becher, Ashbel, Gera, Naaman, Ehi, Rosh, Muppim, Huppim, and Ard. These were the sons of Rachel, who were born to Jacob: fourteen persons in all. The son of Dan was Hushim. The sons of Naphtali were Jahzeel, Guni, Jezer, and Shillem. These were the sons of Bilhah, whom Laban gave to Rachel his daughter, and she bore these to Jacob: seven persons in all. All the persons who went with Jacob to Egypt, who came from his body, besides Jacob's sons' wives, were sixty-six persons in all. And the sons of Joseph who were born to him in Egypt were two persons. All the persons of the house of Jacob who went to Egypt were seventy.

Genesis 46:8-27

The nation of Israel began with Jacob, his sons, and their offspring, including Joseph and his two sons — seventy in all.

Cattlemen, Not Shepherds

Then he sent Judah before him to Joseph, to point out before him the way to Goshen. And they came to the land of Goshen. So Joseph made ready his chariot and went up to Goshen to meet his father Israel; and he presented himself to him, and fell on his neck and wept on his neck a good while. And Israel said to Joseph, "Now let me die, since I have seen your face, because you are still alive." Then Joseph said to his brothers and to his father's household, "I will go up and tell Pharaoh, and say to him, 'My brothers and those of my father's house, who were in the land of Canaan, have come to me. And the men are shepherds, for their occupation has been to feed livestock; and they have brought their flocks, their herds, and all that they have.' So it shall be, when Pharaoh calls you and says, 'What is your occupation?' that you shall say, 'Your servants' occupation has been with livestock from our youth even till now, both we and also our fathers,' that you may dwell in the land of Goshen; for every shepherd is an abomination to the Egyptians."

Genesis 46:28-34

Joseph began to instruct his brothers and his father's household. The Egyptians had a disdain for shepherds, which most in his father's household were. Joseph told them, "When you are asked about your occupation, tell them you have been cattlemen since the days of your youth. It will be better for you if you respond this way."

Stephen's Account Of The Patriarchs

Acts 7 records Stephen's sermon recounting the history of Israel.

"And the nation to whom they will be in bondage I will judge," said God, "and after that they shall come out and serve Me in this place." Then He gave him the covenant of circumcision; and so Abraham begot Isaac and circumcised him on the eighth day; and Isaac begot Jacob, and Jacob begot the twelve patriarchs. And the patriarchs becoming envious, sold Joseph into Egypt. But God was with him and delivered him out of

all his troubles, and gave him favor and wisdom in the presence of Pharaoh, king of Egypt; and he made him governor over Egypt and all his house. Now a famine and great trouble came over all the land of Egypt and Canaan, and our fathers found no sustenance. But when Jacob heard that there was grain in Egypt, he sent out our fathers first. And the second time Joseph was made known to his brothers, and Joseph's family became known to the Pharaoh. Then Joseph sent and called his father Jacob and all his relatives to him, seventy-five people. So Jacob went down to Egypt; and he died, he and our fathers. And they were carried back to Shechem and laid in the tomb that Abraham bought for a sum of money from the sons of Hamor, the father of Shechem.

Acts 7:7-16

Even though Joseph's brothers were moved with envy and sold him into slavery, God went with him and delivered him out of all of his troubles and gave Joseph favor and wisdom in the sight of Pharaoh. Isn't it good to know, even if people are plotting against us and are trying to get rid of us, they cannot get rid of God! God goes with us. He never leaves us. He never forsakes us! Jacob's brothers intended to bring Joseph harm, but God turned it completely around.

Promotion Comes From God

It may look like there is no way you will ever get a raise or a promotion. It may appear that people are holding you down. People may be maligning and accusing you falsely without your knowledge, but you must understand something: they cannot stop a child of God. Promotion does not come from men. Promotion comes from God alone.

I like to pray for people facing impossible situations and hear the reports of how God has delivered them. All of us can probably think back to a time when God brought us out of impossible circumstances. If you're like me, you have probably looked back and thought, "How in the world did God do it?" In the midst of the trouble you think, "Man, if there's anything God can't do, it's got to be this. If there's anything even God is probably scratching His head over, it's got to be this one!" Men can always devise plans, but God can turn those impossible situations around for our good and His glory!

God has a plan for your life, and people cannot overthrow the plan of God! God's plan for your life will come to pass if you continue to walk in faith, patience, and love. Keep committing the situation to the Lord, and you cannot and will not go under!

I once heard a minister say, "I'm like a cork. They can hold me down for so long, but as soon as they let go, I float right back to the top." Whatever circumstances are holding you down, they cannot keep you down! You can expect that, like Joseph, you will float right back to the top!

Chapter 8

The Elder Shall Serve The Younger

The recounting of the life Joseph is the longest story recorded in the book of Genesis, even longer than the account of Abraham's life. It is a very simple story filled with profound truths.

Enduring Riches

God desires to bless His people, but only as long as His people keep their eyes on Him. Joseph suffered undeservedly for many years before he was delivered and promoted to second in authority in the land of Egypt. Rather than becoming bitter as a result of all he suffered, Joseph matured spiritually, and his trust in God increased. In fact, through every situation Joseph faced, he kept his eyes on God and grew spiritually. Once God promoted him, once he was prospered and blessed, those blessings were never again taken from him by the enemy. Satan's desire is for us to focus on possessions and remove our attention from God.

Proverbs 8:18 says, "Riches and honor *are* with me, enduring riches and righteousness." Joseph arrived at the place of "enduring riches" in his life. Just like Joseph, we too can reach that place of "enduring riches" in our lives.

Joseph's Brothers Brought Before Pharaoh

> *Then Joseph went and told Pharaoh, and said, "My father*
> *and my brothers, their flocks and their herds and all that they*
> *possess, have come from the land of Canaan; and indeed they*
> *are in the land of Goshen." And he took five men from among*
> *his brothers and presented them to Pharaoh. Then Pharaoh*
> *said to his brothers, "What is your occupation." And they said*
> *to Pharaoh, "Your servants are shepherds, both we and also*
> *our fathers."*
>
>

Genesis 47:1-3

In the previous chapter, Joseph advised his brothers to tell Pharaoh they were cattlemen rather than shepherds when he asked them about their occupation, because the Egyptians despised shepherds. His brothers did not heed Joseph's advice.

> *And they said to Pharaoh, "We have come to dwell in the land,*
> *because your servants have no pasture for their flocks, for the*
> *famine is severe in the land of Canaan. Now therefore, please*
> *let your servants dwell in the land of Goshen." Then Pharaoh*
> *spoke to Joseph, saying, "Your father and your brothers have*
> *come to you. The land of Egypt is before you. Have your father*
> *and brothers dwell in the best of the land; let them dwell in the*
> *land of Goshen. And if you know any competent men among*
> *them, then make them chief herdsmen over my livestock."*
>
>

Genesis 47:4-6

Pharaoh responded to the brothers, instructing Joseph to allow his father and brothers to live in the best of the land available in Goshen. He continued by basically saying, "I would prefer them to be rulers over the cattle rather than the sheep. It will be in keeping with the custom of the land."

At the end of verse 6 Pharaoh said, "And if you know any competent men among them, then make them chief herdsmen over my livestock." The Greek word for "competent" in this passage is *chayil*, which means "wealth, virtue, valor, strength." Pharaoh said, "Just pick one of your brothers with integrity to be the head herdsman over all of my cattle."

It is interesting to note Joseph didn't recommend any of his brothers for the task. Joseph may have been reflecting on the time when his father sent him to check on his brothers and their flocks. Along the way, Joseph had encountered a man who told him he overheard his brothers saying they were headed to Dothan. Dothan was the direction of the desert. Sheep cannot graze in the desert. The brothers were displaying their irresponsibility. Joseph was probably also remembering how his brothers threw him in a pit and sold him into slavery. I can imagine Joseph scratching his head and saying, "Pharaoh, I wish you hadn't asked me that, because I don't know if I can recommend any of them to watch over cattle." He had not seen integrity in the lives of his brothers.

Jacob Brought Before Pharaoh

Then Joseph brought in his father Jacob and set him before Pharaoh; and Jacob blessed Pharaoh. Pharaoh said to Jacob, "How old are you?" And Jacob said to Pharaoh, "The days of the years of my pilgrimage are one hundred and thirty years; few and evil have been the days of the years of my life, and

117

they have not attained to the days of the years of the life of my
fathers in the days of their pilgrimage."

Genesis 47:7-9

Joseph took his father in to meet with Pharaoh. Jacob blessed Pharaoh. When Pharaoh asked Jacob his age, Jacob responded "few and evil have been the years of my life." Jacob could have been rejoicing in the two wives and twelve sons God had blessed him with or in the fact that his son, Joseph, was alive. Joseph was physically standing right next to him; he was not dead as Jacob had presumed for so many years. However, after being reunited with his beloved son, just learning his needs would be completely supplied with the very best of the land, and sitting in the presence of the ruler of Egypt, Jacob complained to Pharaoh that his life had been unhappy and miserable. He might have said, "I've had some bad days in the past, but God surely has proven Himself faithful. He has greatly blessed my life through you, Pharaoh!"

How often have we focused on the negative things that happened in our lives rather than focused on God and all of the times He delivered us out of them? We have a choice. We can keep our attention on the tribulations or on the victories God has brought us through! Psalm 34:19 says, "Many *are* the afflictions of the righteous, but the LORD delivers him out of them all."

The Land Of Rameses

So Jacob blessed Pharaoh, and went out from before Pharaoh.
And Joseph situated his father and his brothers, and gave them
a possession in the land of Egypt, in the best of the land, in the

land of Rameses, as Pharaoh had commanded.

Genesis 47:10-11

The land of Rameses was a place of blessing for Joseph and his family, but one day it would turn and become a place of cursing for Israel. The children of Israel would become very comfortable in Egypt. We must never become comfortable in the world because it will eventually turn on us. Even though we are in the world, our full trust must be in the Lord.

Four hundred years later, the ruling Pharaoh used the children of Israel, who had become slaves, to build the city of Rameses as a treasure of supply city. Exodus 1:11 says, "Therefore they set taskmasters over them to afflict them with their burdens. And they built for Pharaoh supply cities, Pithom and Rameses." The world will always turn blessing into cursing for you.

Under the Pharaoh of Joseph's day, Israel greatly flourished. They were provided all of the food they could ever need. They had the finest of everything! But somewhere along the way, the children of Israel took their eyes off of God and began to trust in people rather than Him. Regardless of where we are in this life, our trust must always be in God and not in people, because people can disappoint us, even Christian people; but God will never disappoint or fail us. Never!

Tumbleweeds

Jeremiah 17:5-6 says, "Thus says, the LORD: 'Cursed *is* the man who trusts in man and makes flesh his strength, whose heart departs from the LORD. For he shall be like a shrub in the desert, and shall not see when good comes, but shall inhabit the parched places in the wilderness, *in* a salt land *which is* not inhabited."

The word "shrub" refers to a tumbleweed. A tumbleweed has no roots, nor does it have any leaves or fruit. A tumbleweed is at the mercy of the wind; it blows wherever the wind sends it. This passage from Jeremiah says the man whose heart departs from the Lord does not see when good comes and "inhabits the parched places in the wilderness, in a salt land which is not inhabited." Absolutely nothing grows where there is salt. Salt prevents anything from growing.

A Tree Planted By The Waters

Jeremiah 17: 7-8 continues, "*Blessed is* the man who trusts in the LORD, and whose hope is the LORD. For he shall be like a tree planted by the waters, which spreads out its roots by the river, and will not fear when heat comes; but its leaf will be green, and will not be anxious in the year of drought, nor will cease from yielding fruit."

When we trust and hope in the Lord, not only do we have roots that run deep, but we are like a tree that will never wither and will never stop producing fruit! When we're planted by the waters, we can be in a place where there is dryness. We can be in a place where there is a drought and still be fruitful.

I once flew over some drought stricken areas. Everywhere I looked, the terrain was brown where it should have been green. But at one point, we flew over an area with a small river, and on either side of the river, it was green. When the world is in a drought, we can trust in God; we have an endless supply that will never run dry! Our roots continue to grow despite the circumstances, what others say or the world says. Even when drought comes, we have nothing to fear. We are as a tree planted by the waters, we are never dependent on the weather or soil conditions. The "river" is not only the new birth; it is also the Word of God. When we plant ourselves beside this river, our roots will always grow deep.

Psalm 1:1-2 says, "*Blessed is* the man who walks not in the counsel of the ungodly, nor stands in the path of sinners, nor sits in the seat of the scornful; But his delight *is* in the law of the LORD, and in His law he meditates day and night." "The law of the LORD," in verse 2, refers to the Word of God.

Verse 3 says, "He shall be like a tree planted by the rivers of water, that brings forth its fruit in its season, whose leaf also shall not wither; and whatever he does shall prosper." Jeremiah tells us to trust in the Lord. Psalm 1 tells us to trust in His Word, and verse 3 of this psalm says that whatever the person who trusts in the Lord and His Word does will prosper.

While Israel was in Egypt, they began to put their trust in men and became like a tumbleweed — dry, producing no fruit, and blown about by circumstances. When we put our trust in men, we begin to lose our roots. With no roots to hold us in place, we break from our foundation and find ourselves at the mercy of whatever circumstances come along. Circumstances blow us here and there. Sadly, many Christians today do not know how to follow God; they are constantly blown about by the circumstances in their lives. "I don't feel like going to this church anymore." "I don't feel like going to church today." There are many who are professing Christians, but they look just like the world in their actions and choices. They have no consistency in their lives because their roots are not in the Word of God.

The world is getting farther and farther away from the things of God. In a land full of drought, Christians flourish. Often, we aren't even aware of what we walk in daily. Everywhere we go, we're at peace. Everywhere we go, we're established. Everywhere we go, we're content. Everywhere we go, we are stabilized. Why? Because of the river of water that abides in us!

Then Joseph provided his father, his brothers, and all his father's household with bread, according to the number in their families. Now there was no bread in all the land; for the famine was very severe, so that the land of Egypt and the land of Canaan languished because of the famine. And Joseph gathered up all the money that was found in the land of Egypt and in the land of Canaan, for the grain which they brought; and Joseph brought the money into Pharaoh's house.

Genesis 47:12-14

Abundant Provision

Verse 12 says Joseph provided his family with bread according to the size of their household, but verse 13 says there was no bread in the entire land because the famine was so severe. Despite the outward circumstances in Egypt, Joseph made sure his family was well cared for and received the finest and best of the land of Egypt. Although the land experienced drought, they were unaffected by it because of Joseph's provision for them. Even after Joseph's death,

Israel would be taken care of. But a day would come when a new Pharaoh would be in power. The Pharaoh of Moses' day feared the children of Israel. Because their population had increased and continued to grow, he feared their sheer numbers would allow them to overtake him and the nation of Egypt.

Joseph Blesses The People And Blesses Pharaoh

So when the money failed in the land of Egypt and in the land of Canaan, all the Egyptians came to Joseph and said, "Give us bread, for why should we die in your presence? For the money has failed." Then Joseph said, "Give your livestock, and I will give you bread for your livestock, if the money is gone." So they brought their livestock to Joseph, and Joseph gave them bread in exchange for the horses, the flocks, the cattle of the herds, and for the donkeys. Thus he fed them with bread in exchange for all their livestock that year. When that year had ended, they came to him the next year and said to him, "We will not hide from my lord that our money is gone; my lord also has our herds of livestock. There is nothing left in the sight of my lord but our bodies and our lands. Why should we die before your eyes, both we and our land? Buy us and our land for bread, and we and our land will be servants of Pharaoh; give us seed, that we may live and not die, that the land may not be desolate." Then Joseph bought all the land of Egypt for Pharaoh; for every man of the Egyptians sold his field, because the famine was severe upon them. So the land became Pharaoh's. And as for the people, he moved them into the cities, from one end of the borders of Egypt to the other end. Only the land of the priests he did not buy; for the priests had rations allotted to them by Pharaoh, and they ate their rations which Pharaoh gave them; therefore they did not sell their lands. Then Joseph said to the people, "Indeed I have bought you and your land this day for Pharaoh. Look, here is seed for you, and you shall sow the land. And it shall come to pass in the harvest that you shall give one-fifth to Pharaoh. Four-fifths shall be your own, as seed for the field and for your food, for those of your households and as food for your little ones." So they said, "You have saved our lives; let us find favor in the sight of my lord, and we will be Pharaoh's servants." And Joseph made it a law over the land of Egypt to this day, that Pharaoh should have one-fifth, except for the land of the priests only, which did not become Pharaoh's.

Genesis 47:15-26

In the next section of this chapter, God's wisdom flowing through Joseph is displayed once again. Joseph had an answer for every problem brought to him by the people during the time of the drought. With two or three years remaining before the drought ended, everyone ran out of money. Of course, there was enough grain to last until the drought came to an end because the people had given twenty percent of their harvest to Joseph during the plentiful years.

The people came to Joseph and asked him to take their livestock in exchange for food, and he gave them food for another year. At the end of that year, the people ran out of food again. They went to Joseph again saying, "We have no more money, and we have sold all of our livestock to you. All we have remaining is our land and our physical beings." They offered to sell their land to Joseph and to be slaves in exchange for food. Joseph bought all of the land from the Egyptians; the land became Pharaoh's and all of the people became willing slaves to him in exchange for food. The only land Joseph didn't buy was the land that belonged to the priests because they were directly allotted food from Pharaoh and did not need to sell their land.

Joseph gave the people seed to plant in the fields. He required one-fifth of their harvest to be given to Pharaoh and allowed the people to keep four-fifths of the harvest for themselves and their families.

By buying the livestock from the people, Joseph relieved them of the burden of feeding their herds and put the entire responsibility to care for them upon himself. By buying the land from the people, Joseph fed the people. Not only had Joseph blessed the people by keeping them alive, he had also blessed Pharaoh by increasing his domain; he now owned all the land and all the livestock.

After the famine was over, the people were so grateful for Pharaoh's benevolence toward them during the famine, they asked Joseph to allow them to be servants to Pharaoh. Joseph then issued a decree for Pharaoh to receive twenty percent of the crops they grew on his land.

Joseph's Pledge To Jacob

So Israel dwelt in the land of Egypt, in the country of Goshen; and they had possessions there and grew and multiplied exceedingly. And Jacob lived in the land of Egypt seventeen years. So the length of Jacob's life was one hundred and forty-seven years. When the time drew near that Israel must die, he called his son Joseph and said to him, "Now if I have found favor in your sight, please put your hand under my thigh, and deal kindly and truly with me. Please do not bury me in Egypt, but let me lie with my fathers; you shall carry me out of Egypt and bury me in their burial place." And he said, "I will do as you have said." Then he said, "Swear to me." And he swore to him. So Israel bowed himself on the head of the bed.

Genesis 47:27-31

After arriving in Egypt, Jacob lived seventeen years longer, until he was 147 years old. Just before he died, he called Joseph to himself, asked him to put his hand under his thigh and pledge to carry his body out of Egypt to be buried in Canaan. It was a common practice in Israel for a man to put his hand under the thigh of another man when making an oath or promise. This is also seen in Genesis 24:2 when Abraham asked the servant of his house to pledge to find a wife for his son, Isaac.

Verse 31 says, "So Israel bowed himself on the head of the bed." This literally means Israel bowed down and worshiped at the head of his bed. Hebrews 11:21 says, "By faith Jacob, when he was dying, blessed each of the sons of Joseph, and worshiped, leaning on the top of his staff." Not only was Jacob at the head of his bed, he was also leaning on his cane while he worshiped.

Jacob Blesses The Sons Of Joseph

Jacob was preparing to bless the two sons of Joseph.

Now it came to pass after these things that Joseph was told, "Indeed your father is sick"; and he took with him his two sons, Manasseh and Ephraim.

Genesis 48:1

Joseph wanted his sons to be blessed by Jacob before his father died.

And Jacob was told, "Look, your son Joseph is coming to you"; and Israel strengthened himself and sat up on the bed.

Genesis 48:2

Jacob had been lying down, but when he was told Joseph was coming to see him, he sat up on his bed.

Then Jacob said to Joseph: "God Almighty appeared to me at Luz in the land of Canaan and blessed me, and said to me, 'Behold, I will make you fruitful and multiply you, and I will make of you a multitude of people, and give this land to your descendants after you as an everlasting possession.'"

Genesis 48:3-4

The Hebrew phrase Jacob used for "God Almighty" is *El Shaddai*, which translated means "the many breasted one" or "all sufficient one." Even though Jacob lived much of his life in fear and not in faith, the nearer he was to death, the more spiritual he became. He began to reflect upon his life and was reminded how faithful God had been to him; rather than focusing on all of the bad he had encountered in life, he remembered all of the blessings. He was a different man than he had been when he first entered Egypt. As Joseph brought his sons to be blessed by Jacob, he was now in the right place in his relationship with the Lord.

Jacob remembered when the Lord appeared to him many years before in Luz and promised he would be fruitful and multiplied and blessed. He realized God had caused His word to come to pass in his life. Jacob had observed his people multiply exceedingly. But the place God had promised to multiply Jacob and his descendants was in the land of Canaan, not Egypt. God promised he and his descendants would have the land forever.

Jacob realized that while God multiplied his descendants in the land of Egypt, they would ultimately return to Canaan as an entire nation. That was one of the reasons Jacob wanted to be buried in Canaan.

Jacob's Eyes Dimmed By Age

Further down in the chapter, it is revealed that Jacob could not properly identify his grandsons. Because of his age, he had difficulty seeing.

> *Then Israel saw Joseph's sons, and said, "Who are these?" And Joseph said to his father, "They are my sons, whom God has given me in this place." And he said, "Please bring them to me, and I will bless them." Now the eyes of Israel were dim with age, so that he could not see. Then Joseph brought them near to him, and he kissed them and embraced them. And Israel said to Joseph, "I had not thought to see your face; but in fact, God has also shown me your offspring!" So Joseph brought them from beside his knees, and he bowed down with his face to the earth. And Joseph took them both, Ephraim and with his right hand toward Israel's left hand, and Manasseh with his left hand toward Israel's right hand, and brought them near him. Then Israel stretched out his right hand and laid it on Ephraim's head, who was the younger, and his left hand on*

Manasseh's head, guiding his hands knowingly, for Manasseh was the firstborn.

Genesis 48:8-14

Verse 12 says, "Joseph brought them from beside his knees." Literally, this means Joseph set his sons on his father's knees. Jacob laid his right hand on Ephraim's head, who was the younger of the two brothers. Joseph had set his sons on his father's knees according to their ages. According to Jewish tradition, the older son always received the blessing; the right hand was the hand of blessing. Joseph had placed them in a way that his father would place his right hand of blessing on Manasseh, his older son.

Jacob Crossed His Hands

Jacob could not distinguish the difference between his two grandsons, but he was being guided by the Holy Spirit. He crossed his hands and placed his right hand on Ephraim's head.

And he blessed Joseph, and said: "God, before whom my fathers Abraham and Isaac walked, the God who has fed me all my life long to this day, the Angel who has redeemed me from all evil, Bless the lads; Let my name be named upon them, and the name of my fathers Abraham and Isaac; and let them grow into a multitude in the midst of the earth." Now when Joseph saw that his father laid his right hand on the head of Ephraim, it displeased him; so he took hold of his father's hand to remove it from Ephraim's head to Manasseh's head. And Joseph said to his father, "Not so, my father, for this one is the firstborn; put your right hand on his head." But his father refused and said, "I know, my son, I know. He also shall become a people, and he also shall be great; but truly his younger brother shall be greater than he, and his descendants shall become a multitude of nations."

Genesis 48:15-16

When Joseph realized what had happened, he tried to correct things. But Jacob refused.

The Elder Shall Serve The Younger

Jacob's action was part of the fulfillment of what God had spoken to his mother, Rebecca. In Genesis 25:22-23: "But the children struggled together within her; and she said 'If *all is* well, why *am I like* this?' So she went to inquire of the LORD. And the LORD said to her: 'Two nations *are* in your womb, two peoples shall be separated from your body; *one* people shall be stronger than the other, and the older shall serve the younger.'"

Esau, who was the firstborn, served Jacob who was the younger. Jacob came out of his mother's womb hanging onto Esau's heel and for most of his life, he was hanging on to others in an attempt to receive their blessings. When he finally came to the end of his life, God made a great nation of Jacob. The nation of Israel was not named after Esau, the firstborn; it was named after Jacob (Israel). From Esau descended a tribe of heathen Gentiles, not Jews.

Throughout the Bible we see the elder serving the younger. Seth ruled over Cain. Isaac ruled over Ishmael. Jacob ruled over Esau, and now Ephraim would rule over Manasseh.

The Great Exchange

In verse 16, Jacob makes reference to "the Angel" who redeemed him from "all evil." The word "Angel" begins with a capital "a" and refers to the "Angel of the Lord." It was the same "Angel of the Lord" whom Jacob wrestled with. The "Angel of the Lord" is the Lord Jesus Christ. How many of us wrestled with Him for years before finally surrendering our lives to Him?

Jacob crossed his hands and gave Joseph's younger son the greater blessing. This was actually a prophecy about Jesus going to the cross. He was the firstborn son, but when He went to the cross, God crossed His hands and He put His left hand on Jesus and His right hand on us. The blessings that should have gone to Jesus came to us! Jesus, the firstborn, gave us all of the blessings that should have gone to Him! That is the entire essence of 2 Corinthians 5:21, "For He made Him who knew no sin *to be* sin for us, that we might become the righteousness of God in Him."

God simply crossed His hands! The great exchange!

So he blessed them that day, saying, "By you Israel will bless, saying, 'May God make you as Ephraim and as Manasseh!'" And thus he set Ephraim before Manasseh. Then Israel said to Joseph, "Behold, I am dying, but God will be with you and bring you back to the land of your fathers. Moreover I have given to you one portion above your brothers, which I took from the hand of the Amorite with my sword and my bow."
Genesis 48:20-22

The end of Jacob's life far outshined the majority of his life because of his sensitivity to the Holy Spirit. Prior to his death, Jacob accurately prophesied over all of his 12 sons, which will be explored in the next chapter.

Chapter 9

Jacob's Final Words To His 12 Sons

We have come to the end of Jacob's life, and he was a changed man. He was a man fully trusting in the Lord and just before he died, he prophesied over his sons. These sons represent the 12 tribes of Israel. Even so, these brothers had issues. They had rivalry among themselves along with prejudice and prideful hearts. They were self-centered, committed sins, and like us, were imperfect people. In reading about their lives, we may wonder how God could ever use them, but then we must wonder how He could ever use us! We serve the God who can turn cursing into blessing. If we are headed in the wrong direction, He always has blessing waiting for us if we change our attitude and head in the right direction!

Jacob Prophesies To His Sons

Jacob was at the point of death. He had just prophesied over Joseph's sons, and now he asked his sons to gather around him so he could prophesy over them about the future.

And Jacob called his sons and said, "Gather together, that I may tell you what shall befall you in the last days: Gather together and hear, you sons of Jacob, and listen to Israel your father."
Genesis 49:1-2

Reuben

Reuben, Jacob's firstborn, is the first son Jacob prophesied over.

Reuben, you are my firstborn, my might and the beginning of my strength, the excellency of dignity and the excellency of power. Unstable as water, you shall not excel, because you went up to your father's bed; then you defiled it — He went up to my couch.

Genesis 49:3-4

As the firstborn, Reuben was given of certain privileges. In those days, the firstborn always received three entitlements: the rulership, the priesthood, and the double portion. By nature of being the firstborn son, Reuben was originally designated to rule over the entire household, to serve as priest of the home, and to receive a double blessing over the other sons. However, Reuben sinned, which changed the order of things.

Genesis 35:22 records Reuben's sin: "And it happened, when Israel dwelt in that land, that Reuben went and lay with Bilhah his father's concubine; and Israel heard *about it*." This sin was the door that allowed a curse to come into Reuben's life. Because of this sin, he lost all three privileges of being the firstborn of Jacob. Reuben's rulership was given to Judah, his priesthood was given to Levi, and his double portion was given to Joseph.

As previously discussed, Reuben was noble but unstable. He tried unsuccessfully to come up with a plan to rescue Joseph from the pit his other brothers had thrown him in, before they sold him into slavery.

As Jacob is now prophesying at the end of his life, he says, "Reuben, you are my firstborn, my might and the beginning of my strength, the excellency of dignity and the excellency of power." In other words, "Reuben, as my first son, it was intended that you would be the first in rank and power in the family."

But in verse 4, Jacob states the problem, "Unstable as water, you shall not excel, because you went up to your father's bed; then you defiled it—He went up to my couch." The character flaw found in Reuben was when the going got tough, he backed down from doing the right thing; he gave into the pressure confronting him. He was noble until pressure came. He had great ideas but no follow-through. When facing temptation over his father's concubine, he yielded to temptation. He was probably someone who could preach a good sermon against adultery or fornication, but when tempted, committed the sin rather than fled from it.

Simeon And Levi

After speaking over Reuben, Jacob addressed Simeon and Levi.

Simeon and Levi are brothers; instruments of cruelty are in their dwelling place. Let not my soul enter their council; Let not my honor be united to their assembly; For in their anger they slew a man, and in their self-will they hamstrung an ox. Cursed be their anger, for it is fierce; and their wrath, for it is cruel! I will divide them in Jacob and scatter them in Israel.
Genesis 49:5-7

In my opinion, Simeon and Levi were two of the worst of the twelve brothers. They were the second and third sons of Jacob

135

and Leah. These two were always in trouble and would plot evil against others.

In Genesis 34, a story is told about Dinah, the sister of Simeon and Levi. She had gone to visit some young women in the area, and when a prince from that area saw Dinah, he grabbed and raped her. The prince, Shechem, asked his father to make arrangements for Dinah to become his bride. Jacob, Dinah's father, heard about what had happened to his daughter but said nothing to his sons until they returned from the fields where they were herding their livestock.

Hamor, the father of the prince, tried to intercede on behalf of his son to make things right with Jacob. In verses 11-12, his son made an appeal, "Let me find favor in your eyes, and whatever you say to me I will give. Ask me ever so much dowry and gift, and I will give according to what you say to me; but give me the young woman as a wife." The father of this young man had a good heart. He felt truly awful about what his son had done to Dinah and was trying to work things out.

Verse 13 said that Jacob's sons responded deceitfully to Shechem's appeal. In response, they asked for all of the men in their town to be circumcised. If they did not agree, the deal was off. So Hamor and Shechem agreed to the conditions laid out by the sons of Jacob. On the third day, after all of the men had been circumcised and were in pain, Simeon and Levi boldly entered the town and murdered every male and then plundered the city. They took everything and ransacked every house. They then took the remaining wives and daughters as captives.

Jacob was humiliated by what his sons had done. They caused

him great shame among the people. Genesis 34:30 says, "Then Jacob said to Simeon and Levi, 'You have troubled me by making me obnoxious among the inhabitants of the land, among the Canaanites and the Perizzites; and since *I am* few in number, they will gather themselves against me and kill me. I shall be destroyed, my household and I.'"

In addition to lying and killing, Simeon and Levi were cruel. Remember the words of Genesis 49:5: "Simeon and Levi are brothers; instruments of cruelty are in their dwelling place." By this statement, Jacob meant whenever Simeon and Levi came together, they devised a plot for cruelty.

Verse 6 continued, "Let not my soul enter their council; Let not my honor be united to their assembly." Jacob was referring to the secret plot of Simeon and Levi to slay Hamor, Shechem, and all of the men of their village.

At the end of verse 6, Jacob says, "For in their anger they slew a man, and in their self-will they hamstrung an ox." The cruelty of Simeon and Levi was in the description of what they did to the oxen. They cut the thighs of the oxen and allowed them to bleed slowly and painfully; it was nothing but cruel.

Jacob concluded in verse 7, "Cursed be their anger, for it is fierce; and their wrath, for it is cruel! I will divide them in Jacob and scatter them in Israel." Jacob is literally stating that the anger displayed by Simeon and Levi was wrong and indefensible. Jacob never forgot what his sons had done. As a result of this act, Jacob prophesied they would be separated from one another, which happened immediately. They would also be scattered, which would happen later when the time came for them to inherit the land.

Joshua 13:14 describes what happened to Levi and his tribe, "Only to the tribe of Levi he had given no inheritance; the sacrifices of the Lord God of Israel made by fire *are* their inheritance, as He said to them."

Joshua 19:1 describes what happened to Simeon.

The second lot came out for Simeon, for the tribe of the children of Simeon according to their families. And their inheritance was within the inheritance of the children of Judah. They had in their inheritance Beersheba (Sheba), Moladah, Hazar Shual, Balah, Ezem, Eltolad, Bethul, Hormah, Ziklag, Beth Marcaboth, Hazar Susah, Beth Lebaoth, and Sharuhen: thirteen cities and their villages; Ain, Rimmon, Ether, and Ashan: four cities and their villages; and all the villages that were all around these cities as far as Baalath Beer, Ramah of the South. This was the inheritance of the tribe of the children of Simeon according to their families. The inheritance of the children of Simeon was included in the share of the children of Judah, for the share of the children of Judah was too much for them. Therefore the children of Simeon had their inheritance within the inheritance of that people.

Joshua 19:1-9

Simeon and his tribe received no land of their own, just as Jacob prophesied. The land allotted to the tribe of Simeon came from a portion of Judah's inheritance because they received more land than they needed. The tribe of Simeon would be scattered among the people of Judah.

When Simeon and Levi were separated from one another, Levi repented. When we have hearts that are repentant, God can turn cursing into blessing. Even though Levi didn't inherit any land, the blessing he received became a blessing to every tribe. Levi became the priestly tribe and received one-tenth of the income from all of the other tribes.

Numbers 18:20-21 describes Levi's portion. "Then the LORD said to Aaron: 'You shall have no inheritance in their land, nor shall you have any portion among them; I am your portion and your inheritance among the children of Israel. Behold, I have given the children of Levi all the tithes in Israel as an inheritance in return for the work which they perform, the work of the tabernacle of meeting.'"

Levi literally became blessed in Moses and Aaron; both were descendants of the tribe of Levi. Even though Levi was cursed by Jacob, he became blessed because he repented. God basically said to Levi, "Instead of receiving land as your portion, I will be your portion. You will work around the things of God all day long!"

In Deuteronomy 33, Moses prophesied over the tribes of Israel before they entered the land. His prophecy was identical to Jacob's prophesy over the tribes with the exception of Levi, because by the time of Moses' prophecy, Levi had repented.

And of Levi he said: "Let Your Thummim and Your Urim be with Your holy one, whom You tested at Massah, and with whom You contended at the waters of Meribah, who says of his father and mother, 'I have not seen them'; nor did he acknowledge his brothers, or know his own children; for they have observed Your word and kept Your covenant. They shall teach Jacob Your judgments, and Israel Your law. They shall put incense before You, and a whole burnt sacrifice on Your altar. Bless his substance, LORD, and accept the work of his hands; strike the loins of those who rise against him, and of those who hate him, that they rise not again."

Deuteronomy 33:8-11

Moses said to the tribe of Levi, "Not only will you be in God's presence day and night, you will be entrusted with the Thummim and the Urim." The Thummim and Urim were stones the priests used to receive guidance from God for all of the other tribes of Israel.

Judah

Judah was the fourth-born son of Jacob and Leah.

Judah, you are he whom you brothers shall praise; Your hand shall be on the neck of your enemies; Your father's children shall bow down before you. Judah is a lion's whelp; from the prey, my son, you have gone up. He bows down, he lies down as a lion; and as a lion, who shall rouse him?

Genesis 49:8-9

The name Judah means "praise." Literally Judah means "He shall be praised." Judah was the son who was given the rulership as a result of Reuben's sin.

Verse 8 is a prophecy about a future event: the second coming of the Lord Jesus Christ. Judah has yet to be praised by his brothers. This also provides a clue that Judah will be favored among all the tribes because the other tribes will bow down and praise the tribe of Judah. The One who descends from the tribe of Judah is the Lord Jesus Christ, and one day we will all bow down to Him. This prophecy will not be fulfilled until the second coming of the Lord Jesus Christ; all the tribes of Israel will bow down on that day. "Every knee shall bow and every tongue shall confess Jesus as Lord."

Genesis 49:8 states, "Your hand *shall* be on the neck of your enemies." This is a reference to the cross, where Satan was defeated by the Lord Jesus Christ. Ultimately, this passage refers to the death, burial, and resurrection of our Lord Jesus Christ. In 1 John 3:8, we are told, "For this purpose the Son of God was manifested, that He might destroy the works of the devil."

Hebrews 2:14-15 says, "Inasmuch then as the children have partaken of flesh and blood, He Himself likewise shared in the same, that through death He might destroy him who had the power of death, that is, the devil, and release those who through fear of death were all their lifetime subject to bondage." Jesus came to destroy the works of the devil.

Judah is a lion's whelp; from the prey, my son, you have gone up. He bows down, he lies down as a lion; and as a lion, who shall rouse him?

Genesis 49:9

A lion's whelp refers to a young lion; a lion full of strength. In Verse 9, Jacob simply stated that Judah would be the strongest of all the tribes. Just as a young lion in the prime of his strength is called "the king of the beasts," this describes the tribe of Judah. In Revelation 5:5, Jesus is called "the Lion of the tribe of Judah."

Verse 9 says, "He bows down ." The King James Version reads, "He stooped down, he couched as a lion, and as an old lion; who shall rouse him up?" Literally, this prophecy was saying that the tribe of Judah would lie down for a long time before it ever rose up again. Judah would be as an old lion that no longer roused from a lying position, leaving that to the younger lions. From the point Israel went into captivity in Babylon until the second coming of Jesus Christ, no one from the tribe of Judah has or will sit on the throne. After Israel went into captivity, the tribe of Judah had priests and governors over nations but never another king. The last king who sat upon the throne of Judah was Zedekiah. Zedekiah was killed as Israel went into captivity.

> *The scepter shall not depart from Judah, nor a lawgiver from between his feet, until Shiloh comes; And to Him shall be the obedience of the people.*
>
> *Genesis 49:10*

Verse 10 says, "The scepter shall not depart from Judah." Even though the tribe of Judah has not had a ruler since the time of the captivity, God has never removed the scepter from its hand because the next ruler is the Lion of the Tribe of Judah. Jesus will sit on the throne of His father David!

Psalm 89:3-4 says, "I have made a covenant with My chosen, I have sworn to My servant David: 'Your seed I will establish forever, and build up your throne to all generations.' Selah."

The "scepter" refers to the line of kings that would come from the tribe of Judah, including King David and his lineage. Because Judah was the tribe designated to rule, lands were conquered and enemies were placed under their feet.

Verse 10 continues, ". . . nor a lawgiver from between his feet, until Shiloh comes." The meaning of the word *Shiloh* is "peacemaker." The word *shalom* also comes from the root of this word. The peacemaker is the Lord Jesus Christ! He is the Prince of Peace (Isaiah 9:6).

The last part of verse 10 says, "And unto him shall the gathering of the people be." This is a reference to the new birth and to the second advent of the Lord Jesus Christ.

The first time Jesus came, He came as Shiloh — the peacemaker. He will return as the ruler over the whole earth. This will be "the gathering of the people."

> *Binding his donkey to the vine, and his donkey's colt to the choice vine, He washed his garments in wine, and his clothes in the blood of grapes.*
>
> *Genesis 49:11*

The donkey is a reference to an older donkey; it is bound to the vine, the natural nation of Israel. The one doing the binding is Judah. The donkey's colt, a donkey that has never been ridden, refers to the innocence and sinless humanity of the Lord Jesus Christ. The "choice vine" is the Lord Jesus Christ.

Mark 11 refers to when Jesus rode into Jerusalem on a young colt that had never been ridden.

> *Now when they drew near Jerusalem, to Bethphage and Bethany, at the Mount of Olives, He sent two of His disciples; and He said to them, "Go into the village opposite you; and as*

soon as you have entered it you will find a colt tied, on which no one has sat. Loose it and bring it. And if anyone says to you, 'Why are you doing this?' say, 'The Lord has need of it,' and immediately he will send it here." So they went their way, and found the colt tied by the door outside on the street, and they loosed it. But some of those who stood there said to them, "What are you doing, loosing the colt?" And they spoke to them just as Jesus had commanded. So they let them go. Then they brought the colt to Jesus and threw their clothes on it, and He sat on it. And many spread their clothes on the road, and others cut down leafy branches from the trees and spread them on the road. Then those who went before and those who followed cried out, saying: "Hosanna! 'Blessed is He who comes in the name of the Lord!' Blessed is the kingdom of our father David that comes in the name of the Lord! Hosanna in the highest!"

Mark 11:1-10

Mark 11 is a fulfillment of a portion of the prophecy found in Genesis 49:11, but the prophecy continues, "He washed his garments in wine, and his clothes in the blood of grapes." This portion of verse 11 is a reference to the triumphant return of the Lord Jesus Christ at His second coming. He came in innocence the first time, but He will return in power at the second coming. Jesus Christ will return at the Battle of Armageddon.

Revelation 14 describes this battle.

Then I looked, and behold, a white cloud, and on the cloud sat One like the Son of Man, having on His head a golden crown, and in His hand a sharp sickle. And another angel came out of the temple, crying with a loud voice to Him who sat on the cloud, "Thrust in Your sickle and reap, for the time has come for You to reap, for the harvest of the earth is ripe." So He who sat on the cloud thrust in His sickle on the earth, and the earth was reaped. Then another angel came out of the temple which is in heaven, he also having a sharp sickle. And another angel came out from the altar, who had power over fire, and he cried with a loud cry to him who had the sharp sickle, saying, "Thrust in your sharp sickle and gather the clusters of the vine of the earth, for her grapes are fully ripe." So the angel thrust his sickle into the earth and gathered the vine of the earth, and threw it into the great winepress of the wrath of God. And the winepress was trampled outside the city, and blood came out of the winepress, up to the horses' bridles, for one thousand six hundred furlongs.

Revelation 14:14-20

This passage refers to the conquering Lord Jesus Christ! He will tread out the fierceness of His wrath on the earth and will literally stomp upon the nations as someone stomps on grapes, but rather than juice, blood will flow; it will run through the streets of Jerusalem, through the valleys, up to the "horses' bridles." Blood will be so abundant, it will flow like a stream for approximately 180 miles.

Jesus Christ will bring Israel into the millennial reign of the Lord Jesus Christ.

His eyes are darker than wine, and his teeth whiter than milk.

Genesis 49:12

The wine and milk of this verse refer to extreme prosperity. Even though Israel has been prospered in the past, it is nothing in comparison to what they will experience during the Millennium.

First, Armageddon will come when the enemies of Israel will be destroyed, immediately followed by the most glorious time in the history of Israel. They will rule and reign with their "Shiloh," - their "Lawmaker," the Lord Jesus Christ — forever and ever!

Genesis 49:11 says, "He washed his garments in wine, and his clothes in the blood of grapes." Revelation 19 says Christ's robe will be "dipped in blood." Revelation 19 describes the second coming of the Lord Jesus Christ.

> *Now I saw heaven opened, and behold, a white horse. And He who sat on him was called Faithful and True, and in righteousness He judges and makes war. His eyes were like a flame of fire, and on His head were many crowns. He had a name written that no one knew except Himself. He was clothed with a robe dipped in blood, and His name is called The Word of God. And the armies in heaven, clothed in fine linen, white and clean, followed Him on white horses.*
>
> *Revelation 19:11-14*

Verse 14 refers to the "armies in heaven" who will be "clothed in fine linen" following Jesus Christ on "white horses" upon His return. The armies referenced in this verse are us, the redeemed! On that last day, we will simply observe as one man, Jesus Christ, singlehandedly destroys all of the armies of the world. That is the reason His robe will be dipped in blood and ours will be white and clean.

> *Now out of His mouth goes a sharp sword, that with it He should strike the nations. And He Himself will rule them with a rod of iron. He Himself treads the winepress of the fierceness*

and wrath of Almighty God. And He has on His robe and on His thigh a name written: KING OF KINGS AND LORD OF LORDS.

Revelation 19:15-16

This, again, describes what will happen at the second advent of the Lord Jesus Christ. He is our Shiloh! He is our lawgiver! If we have received Jesus Christ as our Lord and Savior, we have already come to Him and have no fear of the wrath that is to come!

Zebulun

The next son Jacob prophesied over was Zebulun.

Zebulun shall dwell by the haven of the sea; He shall become a haven for ships, and his border shall adjoin Sidon.

Genesis 49:13

The name Zebulun means "dwelling place" or "habitation." Jacob foretold that he would inherit the land around the Sea of Galilee and would stretch over to the borders with the Gentiles. Zebulun was strong and steady. He was a comfort to his brothers. He was the stable one, the one his brothers could always come to for help. Joshua 19 describes the inheritance of Zebulun.

The third lot came out for the children of Zebulun according to their families, and the border of their inheritance was as far as Sarid. Their border went toward the west and to Maralah, went to Dabbasheth, and extended along the brook that is east of Jokneam. Then from Sarid it went eastward toward the sunrise along the border of Chisloth Tabor, and went out toward Daberath, bypassing Japhia. And from there it passed along on the east of Gath Hepher, toward Eth Kazin, and extended to Rimmon, which borders on Neah. Then the border went around it on the north side of Hannathon, and it ended in the Valley of Jiphthah El. Included were Kattath, Nahallal, Shimron, Idalah, and Bethlehem: twelve cities with their villages. This was the inheritance of the children of Zebulun according to their families, these cities with their villages.

Joshua 19:10-16

It is interesting that Jesus was raised in the surrounding area of the Sea of Galilee from the age of twelve until He was thirty-three. Joseph and Mary escaped to Egypt with Jesus because a decree had gone forth to kill all of the boys two years and younger, in an attempt to destroy the savior. The Holy Spirit led Joseph, His father, to take Him into the area of Galilee where He was raised. Zebulun's name was fulfilled in the Lord Jesus Christ; the land given to Zebulun as his inheritance became a dwelling place or a habitation for the Lord Jesus Christ himself.

Zebulun's tribe produced excellent soldiers, and in 1 Chronicles 12:33, we see fulfillment of Jacob's prophecy: ". . . of Zebulun there were fifty thousand who went out to battle, expert in war with all weapons of war, stouthearted men who could keep ranks." The stability of Zebulun was manifested in the description of his soldiers: fifty thousand experts in war who could keep ranks. In the face of great opposition, they kept their rank and were brave.

Judges 5:18 says, "Zebulun *is* a people *who* jeopardized their lives to the point of death." The ranks of Zebulun maintained a common purpose when the nation was falling apart. Zebulun could be counted on even when the nation was unstable.

Issachar

The next son Jacob spoke over was Issachar.

Issachar is a strong donkey, lying down between two burdens;
He saw that rest was good, and that the land was pleasant;
He bowed his shoulder to bear a burden, and became a band
of slaves.

Genesis 49:14-15

Issachar was strong-willed and lacked wisdom. He was characterized as a stubborn donkey. Jacob prophesied over Issachar, and what he spoke eventually came to pass.

Verse 14 describes Issachar as "lying down between two burdens." This meant Issachar had a constant battle being waged between his flesh and his spirit; his flesh usually won the battle. The same battle confronts believers today. We are confronted with struggles between the flesh and the spirit. We are to follow after the Spirit. It is a day-by-day choice.

Verse 15 says, "He saw that the rest *was* good, and the land *was* pleasant." Once Issachar came to the land promised and realized how good it was, he decided he wanted rest and prosperity above all else. Issachar would not fight once he arrived in the land.

Verse 15 continues, "He bowed his shoulder to bear a burden, and became a band of slaves." Issachar sold out to his enemies. He lacked wisdom; for him it was peace at any cost. Rather than fighting, he acquiesced to his enemies and once he did, he became

149

a slave to them. This is what happened when he entered the land.

James 1:5-8 says, "If any of you lacks wisdom, let him ask of God, who gives to all liberally and without reproach, and it will be given to him. But let him ask in faith, with no doubting, for he who doubts is like a wave of the sea driven and tossed by the wind. For let not that man suppose that he will receive anything from the Lord; he is a double-minded man, unstable in all his ways." When we lack wisdom, we should ask God for it in faith. This passage says the one who is in doubt is like a wave tossed by the wind. *The King James Version* says we should ask for wisdom "in faith, nothing wavering." Wavering is the battle between the flesh and the spirit. The spirit says, "Believe God," and the flesh says, "Show me evidence. I want proof." This passage says, "Don't vacillate between faith and doubt — between the flesh and the spirit."

Ephesians 4:14 says, "We should no longer be children, tossed to and fro and carried about with every wind of doctrine, by the trickery of men, in the cunning craftiness of deceitful plotting."

A reference to "wind" in the Word of God is either a type of false teaching or a reference to the adversities or storms of life. We are not to be driven by the circumstances of life because they are temporary, just as waves on the sea; they appear momentarily but quickly disappear. James 1 says a man who doubts is like a wave in the sea driven by the wind, double-minded and unstable in all his ways. This man will receive nothing from the Lord.

These passages were a description of the type of man Issachar was. He was unstable, bullheaded, and unwise. He did not ask God for the wisdom he needed and was constantly bouncing back and forth between the flesh and the spirit, between what God might be saying to him and what the circumstances and his natural senses were speaking. Because Issachar tried to buy off his enemies by paying tributes to them, he did not prosper as God intended for him to prosper. Issachar was in a place of prosperity but did not prosper.

Many enter God's Promised Land but never enjoy the land. Many become born again and filled with the Spirit of God but never partake of the blessings of God. Many bring the wilderness into their Promised Land. Many Christians today should be enjoying the blessings of God, but because they are wavering, they are not partaking of the promises.

Issachar entered the Promised Land with the other eleven tribes but didn't enjoy it once he arrived. He saw the beauty of the land. He saw peace and wanted it at any price. Rather than trusting in the Prince of Peace, he relied on his own flesh to pay off his enemies to maintain peace. But the kind of peace Issachar negotiated with his enemies would not be lasting. Issachar became a slave to his enemies.

Dan

Dan shall judge his people as one of the tribes of Israel. Dan shall be a serpent by the way, a viper by the path, that bites the horse's heels so that its rider shall fall backward.
Genesis 49:16-17

Of all of the sons of Jacob, Dan might be considered the worst of the worst. Verse 16 says, "Dan shall judge his people." The word for judge was not meant in a positive way. It means to avenge. Dan will retaliate against the other eleven tribes. This prophecy states that one tribe will rise up in judgment against all of the other tribes. This has yet to come to pass, but it will come to pass as Jacob prophesied. Just as surely as Jesus Christ will return and avenge His enemies at the battle of Armageddon, ushering His people into the millennial reign, this verse of scripture will also come to pass.

Verse 17 says, "Dan shall be a serpent by the way, a viper by the path." A viper is an extremely poisonous snake. This verse continues, "a viper . . . that bites the horse's heels so that its rider shall fall backward." This passage describes Dan as a very poisonous snake just waiting for a horse to pass his way and when it does, he will bite it, causing the horse to rear up and throw the rider off its back.

Numbers 10:25 says of Dan, "Then the standard of the camp of the children of Dan (the rear guard of all the camps) set out according to their armies; over their army *was* Ahiezer the son of Ammishaddai." Dan was the rear guard. When the armies went out to battle, he was always the last one, behind the troops.

The tribe of Dan was the first to go into idolatry, which revealed Dan's tendencies. Judges 18:30-31 says, "Then the children of Dan set up for themselves the carved image; and Jonathan the son of Gershom, the son of Manasseh, and his sons were priests to the tribe of Dan until the day of the captivity of the land. So they set up for themselves Micah's carved image which he made, all the time that the house of God was in Shiloh."

Dan was also the last tribe to receive an inheritance. Joshua 19:47-49 says, "And the border of the children of Dan went beyond these, because the children of Dan went up to fight against Leshem and took it; and they struck it with the edge of the sword, took possession of it, and dwelt in it. They called Leshem, Dan, after the name of Dan their father. This *is* the inheritance of the tribe of the children of Dan according to their families, these cities with their villages. When they had made an end of dividing the land as an inheritance according to their borders, the children of Israel gave an inheritance among them to Joshua the son of Nun."

In 1 Chronicles 27:22, Dan is mentioned last as one of the leaders of the tribes of Israel. In fact, it is not coincidental that Dan is listed last on the list of merits. In the Old Testament, when someone is listed last, there is a reason.

It is also interesting to note that the tribe of Dan is not mentioned as a tribe multiple times in the Bible. In 1 Chronicles chapters 2 through 10, the tribe of Dan is not mentioned as the Bible goes through the genealogies of Israel.

Again in Revelation chapter 7, all of the tribes are listed with the exception of the tribe of Dan. Because of the two half tribes of Ephraim and Manasseh, Joseph's sons, there are thirteen tribes. But in Revelation 7, there are only twelve tribes.

Revelation 7:4-8 says, "And I heard the number of those who were sealed. One hundred *and* forty-four thousand of all the tribes of the children of Israel *were* sealed: of the tribe of Judah twelve thousand *were* sealed; of the tribe of Reuben twelve thousand *were* sealed; of the tribe of Gad twelve thousand *were* sealed; of the tribe of Asher twelve thousand *were* sealed; of the tribe of Naphtali twelve thousand *were* sealed; of the tribe of Manasseh twelve thousand *were* sealed; of the tribe of Simeon twelve thousand *were* sealed;

of the tribe of Levi twelve thousand *were* sealed; of the tribe of Issachar twelve thousand *were* sealed; of the tribe of Zebulun twelve thousand *were* sealed; of the tribe of Joseph twelve thousand *were* sealed; of the tribe of Benjamin twelve thousand *were* sealed."

The tribe of Dan is not mentioned in this passage. Why? No evangelism will come from the tribe of Dan. In fact, I believe, the tribe of Dan will produce the antichrist. He is a snake by the way, one that will rise up in vengeance against all of the other tribes in the Tribulation.

Genesis 49:17 says, "Dan shall be a serpent by the way, a viper by the path, that bites the horse's heels so that its rider shall fall backward." Satan is often referred to as a "serpent." In this instance, the word is a reference to Satan's tool, the antichrist. The horse refers to the nation of Israel during the time of the Tribulation; the rider is the Jewish remnant, the 144,000, which the antichrist will try to destroy.

Revelation 12:13 says, "Now when the dragon saw that he had been cast to the earth, he persecuted the woman who gave birth to the male *Child*." Verse 17 continues, "And the dragon was enraged with the woman, and he went to make war with the rest of her offspring, who keep the commandments of God and have the testimony of Jesus Christ." The dragon is the antichrist and the male child is the 144,000, the remnant that will come from the woman, which is the nation of Israel. The antichrist will rise up through the tribe of Dan and will make war against the remainder of the tribes. In light of this, Genesis 49:16-17 could read, "Dan shall **avenge** his people as one of the tribes of Israel. Dan shall be **the antichrist** by the way, a **poisonous snake** by the path, that bites Israel's heels so that **the Jewish remnant of believers** shall fall backward."

I have waited for your salvation, O Lord!
                                                            Genesis 49:18

Verse 18 is the Jewish remnant during the time of the tribulation, crying out for deliverance from the Lord. Jesus will return, and He will avenge the avenger. He will come against the antichrist and destroy him on that great day!

Gad And Asher

In Genesis 49:19-20, the tribes of Gad and Asher were mentioned.

Gad, a troop shall tramp upon him, but he shall triumph at last. Bread from Asher shall be rich, and he shall yield royal dainties.
                                                            Genesis 49:19-20

Gad and Asher were the two sons of Zilpah. The name Gad means "good fortune."

Verse 19 says, "Gad, a troop shall tramp upon him, but he shall triumph at last." Gad was not kept down by his failures; he rose up from defeat. I like what Gad represents. His life should tell us that we don't need to be defeated by our failures. Gad will be struck down and overcome by the troops around him, but he will rise back up again! Gad is a type of a believer overcome by circumstances who reenters into fellowship with the Lord and rises up again in strength. When we are in fellowship with God, we cannot be kept down. When we are walking by faith, regardless of the circumstances, we will come through victorious!

Verse 20 says, "Bread from Asher shall be rich, and he shall yield royal dainties." Jacob prophesied that Asher would be very prosperous. Asher became one of the most prosperous tribes in Israel, because he was a giver. His life was made very "fat" or prosperous.

Moses, speaking of Asher, prophesied in Deuteronomy 33:24, "Asher *is* most blessed of sons; Let him be favored by his brothers and let him dip his foot in oil." The oil in this verse represents olive oil, which is a symbol of extreme prosperity throughout the Word of God. Again, the tribe of Asher was blessed with prosperity.

Naphtali

Naphtali is a deer let loose; He uses beautiful words.
Genesis 49:21

Naphtali means "my wrestling." He was named in memory of his father Jacob's wrestling match with an angel. The phrase "a deer let loose" meant Naphtali would spring from danger. Even though he was caught like a deer in a trap, he would break loose.

The verse continues, "He uses beautiful words." Naphtali will become one of the evangelistic tribes and will spread the gospel of the Lord Jesus Christ. He will be so appreciative of being set free, he will be compelled to share with others the good news of how to be set free!

Joseph

Verses 22 through 26 speak of the tribe of Joseph. Earlier in our study, we learned that Joseph's tribe was divided into two tribes; the tribe of Ephraim and the tribe of Manasseh.

Joseph is a fruitful bough, a fruitful bough by a well; his branches run over the wall. The archers have bitterly grieved him, shot at him and hated him. But his bow remained in strength, and the arms of his hands were made strong by the hands of the Mighty God of Jacob (from there is the Shepherd, the Stone of Israel), By the God of your father who will help you, and by the Almighty who will bless you with blessings of heaven above, blessings of the deep that lies beneath, blessings of the breasts and of the womb. The blessings of your father have excelled the blessings of my ancestors, up to the utmost bound of the everlasting hills. They shall be on the head of Joseph, and on the crown of the head of him who was separate from his brothers.

Genesis 49:22-26

Joseph was the "double portion" tribe. Jacob gave Joseph a double portion when he blessed his two sons, Ephraim and Manasseh. In this way, Joseph received the double portion that should have gone to Reuben, the first-born, who lost the double portion because of sin.

Verse 22 says, "Joseph *is* a fruitful bough, a fruitful bough by a well; his branches run over the wall." This is a very symbolic verse.

The phrase "a fruitful bough" refers to prosperity. Beyond that, the verse says, "a fruitful bough by a well; his branches run over the wall." This is speaking of the double portion.

The "wall" mentioned refers to protection. In the ancient world, walls were built around an area to protect what was on the inside. God had a protection set up around Joseph and in spite of unjust treatment from others, his "branches" continued to grow over the side of the wall. Joseph was a giver. He cared about people and did what he could to bless others. His branches grew over the wall so other people could partake of the blessings that flowed from his life.

Verse 23 says, "The archers have bitterly grieved him, shot at him and hated him." The "archers" were Joseph's brothers, Potiphar, Potiphar's wife, and ultimately, the devil. Verse 24 continues, "But his bow remained in strength, and the arms of his hands were made strong by the hands of the Mighty *God* of Jacob (from there *is* the Shepherd, the Stone of Israel)." After an arrow is shot, the bow always bounces back. This describes Joseph. Each time pressure came against him, Joseph rebounded.

Joseph didn't turn loose of God's hands. Regardless of what people do to us, when we keep our hands in God's hands, He will keep infusing us with strength. The "hands of the Mighty God" refers to Joseph leaning on the Holy Spirit and the Word of God.

God has placed a "bow" into our hands, and we need to be determined to keep our hands on that bow. That bow is the strength of God — the Word of God. Although other people may shoot at us and even temporarily wound us, if we keep our hands on God's hands, His strength will flow into us. God will cause us to bounce back, which is exactly what happened to Joseph.

The "Shepherd, the Stone of Israel" is the Lord Jesus Christ. Joseph connected to the same God who would bring along the Shepherd and the Stone of Israel; the Lord Jesus Christ.

If God infused strength into the Lord Jesus and caused Him to come, He will surely infuse strength into us. We have the same Father watching over us who watched over Jesus Christ.

We can follow Joseph's example by keeping our eyes on God as Joseph did through every circumstance confronting him.

Verse 24 says, "By the God of your father who will help you, and by the Almighty who will bless you *with* blessings of heaven above, blessings of the deep that lies beneath, blessings of the breasts and of the womb." The term "heaven above" represented spiritual blessings. The phrase "blessings of the deep that lies beneath," referred to blessings that come from the earth. Finally, "blessings of the breasts and of the womb" referred to a posterity that would be blessed even after Joseph was gone. God blessed from the breast and the womb; He gave Joseph his sons, Ephraim and Manasseh. Their tribes not only grew in prosperity but also outnumbered any of the other tribes. Ephraim and Manasseh began as half-tribes, yet they grew to be the largest tribes.

God blessed Joseph. He blessed him spiritually, naturally, and in his family. Joseph could have given up at any point and said, "Forget it. I know I had a dream, but I'm tired. I've been pressured, and I am weary of all of this opposition. I give up." But he did not give up. Instead, he kept his hand in God's hand.

If we choose to do the same, we will discover that the same

God who prospered and blessed Joseph, Ephraim, and Manasseh, is also the One who will bless us! All blessings come from Him; every good and perfect gift comes down from the Father above.

Verse 26 says, "The blessings of your father have excelled the blessings of my ancestors, up to the utmost bound of the everlasting hills. They shall be on the head of Joseph, and on the crown of the head of him who was separate from his brothers." This verse was declaring Joseph's children would be far more blessed than children from the other tribes. The faithfulness of Joseph and the blessings of his life spilled over into the lives of his children. Our faithfulness also spills over into the lives of our children, as do our blessings. The reason Solomon was so blessed was because of the blessing that was on David's life. David was blessed because of the blessings of his father, Jesse. The blessings were multiplied. Joseph was prosperous, but nothing like his sons were as they entered the land promised to them. God tremendously blessed Ephraim and Manasseh as they entered the land. God's blessings are intended to increase from generation to generation.

Benjamin

Verse 27 contains Jacob's word over his youngest son, Benjamin.

Benjamin is a ravenous wolf; in the morning he shall devour the prey, and at night he shall divide the spoil.
Genesis 49:27

The name Benjamin means "son of my right hand." The word ravenous means "to eat rapidly." Jacob compares Benjamin to a ravenous wolf. Just as a wolf tears its prey and consumes it quickly, this describes the tribe of Benjamin. The Benjamites were known throughout the Word of God as a very warlike, aggressive tribe. When they went to battle, they could quickly destroy their enemies. They could go into battle and conquer their enemies in a day! When called to battle, the Benjamites were always put on the front lines. They were fierce warriors.

King Saul of the Old Testament came from the tribe of Benjamin. At the beginning of his life, he was a very strong, courageous warrior. Saul of Tarsus of the New Testament was also from the tribe of Benjamin. He channeled all of the anger and vengeance he originally poured out against the church of the Lord Jesus Christ and turned it against the kingdom of Satan. God used him to write most of the epistles. It makes sense he used terminology related to war in his writings. "The weapons of our warfare are not carnal," "we are more than conquerors," "fight the good fight of faith," "the armor of God," and "the sword of the Spirit," all of this came from a man from the tribe of Benjamin who understood war.

Jacob's Death

After prophesying over his sons, Jacob charged his sons to bury him in the land of Canaan after he died.

All these are the twelve tribes of Israel, and this is what their father spoke to them. And he blessed them; he blessed each one according to his own blessing. Then he charged them and said to them: "I am to be gathered to my people; bury me with my fathers in the cave that is in the field of Ephron the Hittite, in the cave that is in the field of Machpelah, which is before Mamre in the land of Canaan, which Abraham bought with the field of Ephron the Hittite as a possession for a burial place. There they buried Abraham and Sarah his wife, there they buried Isaac and Rebekah his wife, and there I buried Leah. The field and the cave that is there were purchased from the sons of Heth." And when Jacob had finished commanding his sons, he drew his feet up into the bed and breathed his last, and was gathered to his people.

Genesis 49:28-33

Jacob made it clear to his sons that he did not want to be buried in the land of Egypt; he wanted to be buried in the land of Canaan. Jacob was buried soon after his death. Joseph wasn't buried for 400 years. Why did it matter to Jacob where he would be buried? Where we are buried after death really doesn't matter, but Jacob wanted to be buried in Canaan as a memorial for future generations. He also wanted to be buried in Canaan because he believed in the resurrection. Even today, many people want to be buried in Jerusalem because they believe in the resurrection. Those who have been buried on the Mount of Olives have been buried with their feet toward the city of Jerusalem so when the Messiah comes, they will stand up and face the city. Of course, we believe the Messiah has already come and all believers, from every tribe and nation, will be raptured before the second coming of Jesus.

In verse 31 Jacob states, ". . . there (Jerusalem) I buried Leah."

If we remember the story of Jacob, we know he wanted to marry Rachel but had to be tricked into marrying Leah, the eldest daughter of Laban (see Genesis 29:1-30). Rachel was beautiful and Jacob loved her, yet in his death, Jacob wanted to be buried with Leah. Leah produced some of the strongest tribes in Israel.

Verse 33 describes how Jacob died. "And when Jacob had finished commanding his sons, he drew his feet up into the bed and breathed his last, and was gathered to his people."

After sitting on the side of the bed as he prophesied over his sons, Jacob pulled up his feet into the bed and breathed his last breath. What a wonderful way to go! I believe this is the way God wants us to go when the time comes!

Verse 33 concludes concerning Jacob, ". . . and was gathered to his people." Jacob was not gathered to his people when he was buried. He was gathered to his people when he died. Even though Jacob wanted his body buried in a specific place with his people, he was gathered to his people the moment he left this earth!

The moment any believer leaves this earth, they are gathered or reunited with their "people." To be absent from the body is to be present with the Lord! The very moment a believer dies, they are face to face with the Lord and with loved ones who have preceded them in death.

In the case of Jacob, because Jesus had not yet come and had not yet been resurrected, he went to paradise. However, at the resurrection of the Lord Jesus Christ, Jacob was taken to Heaven, which is where he remains today!

Chapter 10

The Bones Of Joseph

The story of Joseph is a profoundly simple story about living the life of faith, persevering regardless of the circumstances, and holding on to the promises of God no matter what is happening around us in the natural.

Joseph could never have imagined how the dream God had given him would be fulfilled; as the years passed, he probably could not picture his brothers ever bowing down to him. It is absolutely incredible how God caused it all to come to pass, how He blessed and delivered that family through Joseph's life. In fact, the entire known world at that time was blessed because of Joseph's life during a time of extreme drought.

A Time Of Mourning

Then Joseph fell on his father's face, and wept over him, and kissed him. And Joseph commanded his servants the physicians to embalm his father. So the physicians embalmed Israel.
Genesis 50:1-2

Immediately after Jacob's death, Joseph wept and kissed his father's face. He called for his servants, the physicians. Joseph had doctors in his home. Some Christians believe it is wrong to consult with physicians, but not only did Joseph have servants who were doctors, later in the New Testament we learn that Luke was a doctor; the Apostle Paul and Luke traveled together spreading the Gospel.

> *Forty days were required for him, for such are the days required for those who are embalmed; and the Egyptians mourned for him seventy days.*
>
> *Genesis 50:3*

The Egyptians mourned seventy days over the death of Jacob. They had a tremendous love for Jacob as well as his family.

Pharaoh Grants Permission To Bury Jacob In Canaan

> *Now when the days of his mourning were past, Joseph spoke to the household of Pharaoh, saying, "If now I have found favor in your eyes, please speak in the hearing of Pharaoh, saying, 'My father made me swear, saying, "Behold, I am dying; in my grave which I dug for myself in the land of Canaan, there you shall bury me." Now therefore, please let me go up and bury my father, and I will come back.'"*
>
> *Genesis 50:4-5*

Joseph went before Pharaoh and said, "My father made me swear to bury him in Canaan." Joseph was an honest man. Not only was he truthful about his father's request when he went before Pharaoh, he also demonstrated his integrity of heart by making this request of Pharaoh, as he promised his father he would.

> *And Pharaoh said, "Go up and bury your father, as he made you swear." So Joseph went up to bury his father; and with him went up all the servants of Pharaoh, the elders of his house,*

*and all the elders of the land of Egypt, as well as all the house
of Joseph, his brothers, and his father's house. Only their little
ones, their flocks, and their herds they left in the land of Goshen.
And there went up with him both chariots and horsemen, and
it was a very great gathering.*

Genesis 50:6-9

Mourning And Memorial

A very large multitude of both Egyptians and Israelites went
with Joseph to bury his father in Canaan. Not only did Joseph's
brothers and their households travel to Canaan, so did all of the top
officials of Pharaoh's household and of Egypt. Only the children
and the flocks and herds of Joseph's brothers remained in Egypt
during this time.

*Then they came to the threshing floor of Atad, which is beyond
the Jordan, and they mourned there with a great and very
solemn lamentation. He observed seven days of mourning for
his father.*

Genesis 50:10

Joseph and the multitude came to the threshing floor of Atad.
The name Atad means "thorns." I personally believe the threshing
floor of Atad is a type of the crucifixion and resurrection of Jesus
Christ. There was a very solemn memorial service and observation
for Jacob that lasted seven days.

*And when the inhabitants of the land, the Canaanites, saw
the mourning at the threshing floor of Atad, they said, "This*

is a deep mourning of the Egyptians." Therefore its name was called Abel Mizraim, which is beyond the Jordan.

Genesis 50:11

This passage states that the Canaanites saw the mourning of the people. It is important to note that this was the last time the Canaanites would see the children of Israel until they returned from their captivity in Egypt 470 years later. In thirty years, Israel would go into captivity for 400 years, and once they were released, they wandered in the wilderness for forty years.

It was mentioned previously that Israel began as 75 people, but by the time they were released from captivity in Egypt, they were over two million strong! Even though Joseph had favor with Pharaoh, in just thirty years, there would be a new Pharaoh who did not remember Joseph.

The inhabitants of the land noticed the deep mourning of the Egyptians. The name Abel Mizraim means "the mourning of the Egyptians."

Jacob Is Buried With His Ancestors

So his sons did for him just as he had commanded them. For his sons carried him to the land of Canaan, and buried him in the cave of the field of Machpelah, before Mamre, which Abraham bought with the field from Ephron the Hittite as property for a burial place.

Genesis 50:12-13

Jacob's sons honored his request to be buried with his ancestors.

Verse 13 says Jacob's sons buried him in a cave in the field of Machpelah. The name Machpelah means "double." Abraham purchased this cave in Hebron as a burial place.

Genesis 23 recounts the purchase of this land. Genesis 23:7-9 says, "Then Abraham stood up and bowed himself to the people of the land, the sons of Heth. And he spoke with them, saying, "If it is your wish that I bury my dead out of my sight, hear me, and meet with Ephron the son of Zohar for me, that he may give me the cave of Machpelah which he has, which *is* at the end of his field. Let him give it to me at the full price, as property for a burial place among you." Verses 17-18 say, "So the field of Ephron which *was* in Machpelah, which was before Mamre, the field and the cave which was in it, and all the trees that *were* in the field, which *were* within all the surrounding borders, were deeded to Abraham as a possession in the presence of the sons of Heth, before all who went in at the gate of his city."

Sarah was buried in this cave and later Abraham, Isaac, Rebekah, and Leah were buried in this same place.

Joseph's Brothers Misjudge His Heart

And after he had buried his father, Joseph returned to Egypt, he and his brothers and all who went up with him to bury his father. When Joseph's brothers saw that their father was dead, they said, "Perhaps Joseph will hate us, and may actually repay us for all the evil which we did to him."

Genesis 50:14-15

The perspective of Joseph's brothers was a reflection of their hearts. While their father was alive, they felt like he was a protection from Joseph's wrath being poured out on them for what they had done to him. They had no understanding of the forgiveness and mercy of God. They believed Joseph would respond to them in the way they would have responded to him, had the tables been turned. But Joseph's heart was pure and his forgiveness genuine.

> *So they sent messengers to Joseph, saying, "Before your father died he commanded, saying, 'Thus you shall say to Joseph: "I beg you, please forgive the trespass of your brothers and their sin; for they did evil to you."' Now, please, forgive the trespass of the servants of the God of your father." And Joseph wept when they spoke to him.*
>
> *Genesis 50:16-17*

It is true, Jacob requested that his sons bury him in Canaan, but he never told them to ask Joseph to forgive them for what they had done to him years before. They lied! Even though they had lived around Joseph for many years, they had not changed. They were operating in fear. They had experienced God's grace for years, but still had no understanding of it. Joseph had consistently showed his brothers love and treated them with the same grace God had extended to him. Joseph's brothers had failed time and time again, but Joseph continued to love and care for them, had given them a home and possessions, and had given them peace and safety. Still, they wrongly judged his heart's motives.

In talking among themselves, the brothers became convinced that the only reason Joseph treated them well was because their father had been alive. They had it all figured out. They were certain Joseph would retaliate against them, so they sent a servant to him with the lie that Jacob had said, "Please forgive my sons of all they did to you back there."

Joseph knew they were lying to him and realized his brothers had not changed. Joseph's response was to weep. He had no bitterness in his heart toward his brothers. Like God, he only wanted what was best for their lives and the lives of their families.

> *Then his brothers also went and fell down before his face, and they said, "Behold, we are your servants."*
> **Genesis 50:18**

Joseph's brothers fell down before him, fearful for their lives. In essence, they begged him, "Please don't kill us! We will be your slaves!"

Joseph was in God's perfect will for his life. He had learned that even when people mistreat us, we can still be in the middle of God's will. Others cannot remove us from His will. They can retaliate against us, but as we stand in faith, God is able to turn adversity and cursing into blessing.

Each time Joseph met opposition, he chose to rejoice in the Lord. He ultimately received the promise of God. He held fast to the dream God had given him. He was sold into slavery, spent thirteen years in prison, and was forgotten for two years by a man God had blessed through Joseph's gift of interpreting dreams. When Joseph was finally brought out of prison to stand before Pharaoh, he was at the lowest point in his life. Little did he know, this would be the moment he would be catapulted to the pinnacle of his life and the fulfillment of God's Word to him!

Joseph Comforts And Blesses His Brothers

Joseph said to them, "Do not be afraid, for am I in the place of God? But as for you, you meant evil against me; but God meant it for good, in order to bring it about as it is this day, to save many people alive. Now therefore, do not be afraid; I will provide for you and your little ones." And he comforted them and spoke kindly to them.

Genesis 50:19-21

Not only did Joseph reassure his brothers that they had nothing to fear, he testified of God's goodness and faithfulness and displayed the kindness, comfort, and provision of God!

So Joseph dwelt in Egypt, he and his father's household. And Joseph lived one hundred and ten years. Joseph saw Ephraim's children to the third generation. The children of Machir, the son of Manasseh, were also brought up on Joseph's knee.

Genesis 50:22-23

Machir was the oldest son of Manasseh. His descendants eventually settled in the land taken from the Amorites. Numbers chapters 27 and 36 describe the Machirites, the descendants of Machir.

Numbers 27:1 says, "Then came the daughters of Zelophehad the son of Hepher, the son of Gilead, the son of Machir, the son of Manasseh, from the families of Manasseh the son of Joseph; and these were the names of his daughters: Mahlah, Noah, Hoglah, Milcah, and Tirzah."

Numbers 36:1 says, "Now the chief fathers of the families of the children of Gilead the son of **Machir**, the son of Manasseh, of the families of the sons of Joseph, came near and spoke before Moses and before the leaders, the chief fathers of the children of Israel.

Joseph lived to be 110 years old, and he was able to watch his grandchildren be raised. At 110 years old, Joseph told his family, "I am dying, but God will surely visit you."

The Fourth Generation

Genesis 15 describes the time when God entered into a covenant relationship with Abram.

In verses 13-15, God spoke to Abram, "Know certainly that your descendants will be strangers in a land *that* is not theirs, and will serve them, and they will afflict them four hundred years. And also the nation whom they serve I will judge; afterward they shall come out with great possessions. Now as for you, you shall go to your fathers in peace; you shall be buried at a good old age. But in the fourth generation they shall return here, for the iniquity of the Amorites is not yet complete."

Joseph knew about the encounter Abram had with God; he knew about the 400 years in captivity and the ultimate release from captivity spoken of by God. He understood that God had prophesied, and it was His will for Joseph to be sent to Egypt. As he watched God work in his life, Joseph realized it was God's will to use him to deliver the Egyptians from the famine and economic collapse. Joseph knew it was God's will for his family to be placed in the land of Goshen for their protection. But Joseph also knew his family and their descendants would eventually return to their own country.

The "fourth generation" mentioned in verse 16 would be the generation of Moses and Joshua. The Amorites mentioned in verse 16, were Canaanites and were the people who observed Joseph, his family, and the Egyptians who returned to bury Jacob. After 400 years, they would once again watch as Israel returned from Egypt to their homeland.

400 Years Of Grace

During the 400 years the children of Israel were in captivity, God dealt with the inhabitants of Canaan about their salvation. For 400 years they repeatedly rejected salvation, and during that time, the population of Israel continued to increase. God always gives grace before judgment. God gave the Canaanites 400 years of grace. During that time, the iniquity of the Amorites continued to increase.

And Joseph said to his brethren, "I am dying; but God will surely visit you, and bring you out of this land to the land of which He swore to Abraham, to Isaac, and to Jacob." Then Joseph took an oath from the children of Israel, saying, "God will surely visit you, and you shall carry up my bones from here." So Joseph died, being one hundred and ten years old; and they embalmed him, and he was put in a coffin in Egypt.

Genesis 50:24-26

The Bones Of Joseph

The children of Israel would remember Joseph's dying words, "God will surely visit you." He asked them to take an oath to carry his bones from Egypt back to Canaan. It should be noted that Joseph's bones were not buried; he was embalmed and placed in a coffin in Egypt.

Exodus 13 explains what happened 430 years after Joseph's death. Exodus 13:19 says, "And Moses took the bones of Joseph with him, for he had placed the children of Israel under solemn oath, saying, 'God will surely visit you, and you shall carry up my bones from here with you.'"

Not only did the children of Israel carry great possessions with them as they left the land of Egypt, they also carried the coffin of Joseph with them. Joseph's coffin had never been buried; it had been left for over 400 years for the Israelites to see, and every time they saw his coffin, it was a reminder of God's promise that they would one day be delivered from Egypt and return to Canaan.

Joseph's Bones

Joshua 24 continues the story. Verse 32 says, "The bones of Joseph, which the children of Israel had brought up out of Egypt, they buried at Shechem, in the plot of ground which Jacob had bought from the sons of Hamor the father of Shechem for one hundred pieces of silver, and which had become an inheritance of the children of Joseph."

Joseph was buried in the land that was divided between his sons, Ephraim and Manasseh. It is also the place where John the Baptist would baptize Jesus.

When we reflect on the life of Joseph, so many great moments come to mind, reflecting his heart and character. He forgave his brothers. He forgave Potiphar and Potiphar's wife. He trusted God to interpret dreams. He ultimately interpreted Pharaoh's dream, which saved the nation of Egypt and the land of Israel. Nations came to Joseph during the famine, and he was able to witness to them during their time of great need. But of all the things Joseph did, one particular event is recorded about him in the book of Hebrews.

In Hebrews 11:22, it is said of Joseph, "By faith Joseph, when he was dying, made mention of the departure of the children of Israel, and gave instructions concerning his bones."

Of all his accomplishments, why were Joseph's bones mentioned? The facts that he walked in forgiveness, was promoted from prison to second in authority in Egypt, or was used to save nations are not mentioned. Why were Joseph's bones so important? Because they were the focal point of the promise that the children of Israel would survive as a nation! For over 400 years, they would be persecuted as a nation. They would become slaves, forced to build treasure cities with bricks made without straw and by their own hands. They would work under the worst of conditions; their male children two and under would be slaughtered during Moses' day. The only Bible the children of Israel had was Joseph's bones! They did not have a scroll they could open each day to read the Scriptures of God. They did not have priests they could talk to about the good things of God. All they had was a coffin and the promise of one day returning to Canaan to bury the bones of Joseph.

The Bones Of Joseph

For 400 years, generation after generation, parents would die, children would be born, mature, and have their own children. They would die, and their children would mature and have more children. Under the most intense persecution, generation after generation would pass by Joseph's coffin. Parents would tell their children, "As long as that coffin is unburied, we have the promise that we will be delivered!" God delivered on that promise! They held fast to that promise for 400 years, and God brought them out!

They carried Joseph's bones out of Egypt and across the Red Sea as they walked on dry ground and the enemy was destroyed. They carried his coffin through the wilderness for forty years while complaining, "Moses, we think you lied to us! We miss Egypt! We don't think God is really going to bring us into that land!" And while they were griping to Moses, someone was carrying that coffin, which had been in Egypt for 400 years attached to the promise, "God will surely visit you, and bring you out of this land to the land of which He swore to Abraham, to Isaac, and to Jacob."

What God Has Spoken Will Surely Come To Pass

Understand this important truth: Regardless of how long it takes for the promises of God to come to pass in our lives; they will come to pass. If God has spoken it, it will come to pass. If God said, "My God shall supply all of your need according to his riches in glory by Christ Jesus" (Philippians 4:19), it doesn't matter if it has been two years or ten years, it *will* come to pass!

If the children of Israel could come through 400 years with one promise, we certainly can make it with sixty-six books and over

3,000 recorded promises of deliverance! We can come through with "I've never seen the righteous forsaken or his seed begging bread" (Psalm 37:25 paraphrased). We can make it on "Cast your burden on the Lord and He will sustain you" (Psalm 55:22 paraphrased), and "God is not a man that he should lie" (Numbers 23:19).

The pinnacle of Joseph's faith was declaring while dying, "God will surely visit you, and you shall carry up my bones from here." When Joseph's bones were finally buried, the children of Israel had arrived in the land God had promised them. They hadn't returned to that land since burying Jacob's body. The Amalekites had observed them then, but now they observed them again as over two million returned in faith, following their leader, Moses.

Imagine as generation after generation explained to their children the story of Joseph. "Son, Joseph was a man who hit rock bottom, and God brought him out and made him to sit next to Pharaoh. God has promised us a land that flows with milk and honey. We will be delivered from Egypt and arrive in the land God has promised!"

The children of Israel faced five years of battles once they entered the land, but they were a changed people. They marched around the walls of Jericho for seven days, and not one of them complained or grumbled. As they marched around the walls, the people of Jericho were probably shouting all types of insults at them. But Israel marched on in faith and on the seventh day, they gave a shout and the walls came down. That was only the beginning. City after city, triumph after triumph, possession after possession, they conquered their enemies and after five years, God blessed them with even more possessions in the land of Canaan than they had when they left Egypt.

You may feel like you are in bondage in "Egypt." You may feel like you are in the "wilderness." Or you may feel like you just "crossed the Red Sea" with battles ahead. Know that God is bringing you through! What you hold in your hand is an "empty coffin." Jesus has risen from the dead! The Bible is still the symbol we hold in our hand. Every time we pass by our Bible, we should realize God has promised deliverance. It doesn't matter what it looks like. It doesn't matter if the bottom has fallen out more than once, and it feels like we're lower than we've ever been before. We must realize, if we've hit bottom, up is the only way out and deliverance is certain!

God's promise to Joseph finally came to pass. He trusted God in the pit. He trusted God as he was carried bound as a slave to Egypt. He trusted God as he was promoted to a position of honor in Potiphar's house. He trusted God when falsely accused by Potiphar's wife. He trusted God while being thrown into prison. He trusted God when he was forgotten by a man he had encouraged. And while he trusted God, he forgave. Joseph trusted God unlike other men who might have harbored unforgiveness and bitterness inside. With purity and complete integrity of heart, Joseph trusted God!

Regardless of where you are in the fulfillment of your promise from God, let the life of Joseph serve as a source of encouragement and inspiration. Trust God through every adversity, false accusation, and lack of support and understanding from others who say God's promise will never come to pass. Trust God! His promise to you will surely come to pass!

Meet Bob Yandian

From 1980 to 2013, Bob Yandian was the pastor of Grace Church in his hometown of Tulsa, Oklahoma. After 33 years, he left the church to his son, Robb, with a strong and vibrant congregation.

During those years, he raised up and sent out hundreds of ministers to churches and missions organizations in the United States and around the world. He has authored over thirty books and established a worldwide ministry to pastors and ministers.

He is widely acknowledged as one of the most knowledgeable Bible teachers of this generation. His practical insight and wisdom into the Word of God has helped countless people around the world to live successfully in every area of the daily Christian life.

Bob attended Southwestern College and is also a graduate of Trinity Bible College. He has served as both instructor and Dean of Instructors at Rhema Bible Training Center in Broken Arrow, Oklahoma.

Bob has traveled extensively throughout the United States and internationally, taking his powerful and easy to apply teachings that bring stability and hope to hungry hearts everywhere. He is called "a pastor to pastors."

Bob and his wife, Loretta, have been married for over forty years, are parents of two married children, and have five grandchildren. Bob and Loretta Yandian reside in Tulsa, Oklahoma.